Royal Albert Hall

Royal Albert Hall

A Celebration in 150 Unforgettable Moments

EBURY
PRESS

Contents

The Royal Albert Hall was originally conceived thanks to the inspiration of Prince Albert, my great-great-Grandfather. Albert was a man of extraordinary vision and ingenuity, and, together with Queen Victoria, he shared his passion for the global arts, education and culture with the nation.

Since its opening in 1871, the Hall has hosted concerts of every conceivable type, charity events, world leaders, meetings, operas, ballets, films, and sports – all with the central aim of promoting the arts and sciences, as Prince Albert intended.

I have been Patron of the Royal Albert Hall since 1953, and my family and I have enjoyed many events including the annual Royal British Legion Festival of Remembrance, the Centenary of the Women's Institute, and even my 92nd Birthday celebration.

As it embarks on its next 150 years, I hope that the Royal Albert Hall will continue to thrive, and that many more people will have the opportunity to make their own memories of this wonderful building.

ELIZABETH R.

BELOW: The opening
ceremony for The Great
Exhibition in 1851,
attended by Queen
Victoria.

1 A ROYAL VISION

For 150 years the Royal Albert Hall has been a jewel amongst London's many iconic buildings. Its architectural beauty draws visitors from across the world, while its versatility allows a vast range of events, from live music, ballet and award shows to boxing, marathons, political debates and even car exhibitions.

Conceived by Queen Victoria's idealistic husband Prince Albert, who dreamed of a 'Central Hall' to promote the arts and sciences, the Hall has been following his royal vision ever since it first opened its doors in 1871.

1. ALBERTOPOLIS

The idea for the Royal Albert Hall was born out of the success of the 1851 Great Exhibition of the Works of Industry of All Nations, two decades earlier. The brainchild of Prince Albert and the civil servant and patron of the arts Henry Cole, the event showcased objects and curios drawn from industries and cultures around the world, in a purpose-built hall constructed from glass and cast iron called the Crystal Palace. Over 15,000 exhibitors from sixty countries displayed 100,000 pieces, including a leech-driven barometer, folding pianos and the largest known diamond in the world, the 186-carat Koh-i-Noor, now part of the Crown Jewels.

Over its six-month run, the Great Exhibition attracted over six million visitors and yielded a profit of £186,000, the equivalent of around £21 million today. Flush with the success of the exhibition, Prince Albert conceived an inspirational vision for a more permanent cultural centre for the entire nation, situated in the heart of London and consisting of didactic museums, scholarly institutions and exhibition spaces.

In 1852, a large swathe of land in Kensington Gore was bought by the Royal

BELOW: A drawing of
the Royal Albert Hall's
south entrance and
Albert Memorial from
the Royal Horticultural
Society Gardens, South
Kensington.

Commissioners for the Great Exhibition of 1851 for the sum of £327,500, with
£177,500 coming from the Government and the remaining £150,000 from
the exhibition's profits. It was quickly dubbed 'Albertopolis', and a year later
the Prince voiced his desire to see a great Central Hall (see page 9) built as the
centrepiece of the complex. Sadly, he was never to see his vision become a reality
as he died of typhoid on 14 December 1861, at the age of forty-two.

2. A GRAND PLAN

The South Kensington Museum – later renamed the Victoria and Albert
Museum – was the first of the many impressive buildings envisaged by Prince
Albert to be completed, and was opened by Queen Victoria in 1857. It was also

BELOW: The re-opening
of the Albert Memorial,
20 October 1998.

The Great Exhibition

The global event opened on 1 May 1851 and ran until October.

The Crystal Palace, designed by Joseph Paxton, was built in Hyde Park and measured 1,848 feet (563 metres) long and 408 feet (124 metres) wide.

At its centre was a central transept that reached a height of 108 feet (33 metres), beneath which was an impressive fountain made from pink glass, which itself stood 27 foot (8 metres) high.

Exhibits were displayed in over ten miles of gallery space, and the building housed the first ever paid-for flushing public conveniences, costing a penny per person, from which the phrase 'spend a penny' derives.

BELOW: A view of the
Hall from Princess Gate,
Kensigton Gardens taken
in the 1940s.

the headquarters of the influential Science and Arts Department, thus marrying these two disciplines in keeping with Albert's wishes.

At the centre of Albertopolis were the Royal Horticultural Society Gardens, at the southern end of which the architect Francis Fowke, a captain in the Royal Engineers, designed an iron and brick gallery to house the ambitious International Exhibition of 1862, which unfortunately proved to be unprofitable. Over the following decades, the Natural History Museum, the Royal College of Music and the Imperial Institute were all built. Following the untimely death of the Prince Consort, which threw both the nation and the Queen into a prolonged state of mourning, a grand memorial was proposed to stand at the head of Albertopolis, in Kensington Gardens, just yards from the site of the proposed Central Hall.

It was estimated that the Albert Memorial, designed by George Gilbert Scott, would cost £100,000, while the Hall would require an additional £250,000. The public and Government were asked for donations for both projects, but only a little over £120,000 was raised, and the idea of the Hall was scrapped.

A Royal Vision

3. RAISING MONEY TO RAISE THE ROOF

Henry Cole was determined that Albert's dream of a Central | Hall would become a reality and, in 1864, he brought in the architect of the South Kensington Museum, Francis Fowke, to design a hall that could seat 7,000. Cole also came up with the ingenious idea of selling seats in the Hall before it was even open at £100 each to fund the project. Each one sold had a 999-year lease and, to encourage more subscribers, the future Edward VII, then the Prince of Wales, was asked to be President of the committee established to procure the design, financing and construction of the Hall.

The Queen backed the plan and told the Royal Commission for the Great Exhibition of 1851 that a Central Hall was an important part of her husband's legacy. As a result, they agreed to pay £50,000 of the £200,000 needed, and also to let the site at a nominal rate – on the condition that the Commission would have the same rights as those a subscriber who bought 500 seats would have.

The Queen and the Prince of Wales were among the first to purchase seats, with Victoria taking twenty in total. In order to facilitate this purchase, two ten-seat grand tier boxes were merged to create the Queen's Box, now owned by Elizabeth II. When the reigning monarch is in the Hall, special chairs from the Hall's Royal Retiring Room are positioned in the box and it is decorated with silk drapes and a 'hammercloth' bearing the royal coat of arms is hung over the front.

Today some 1,268 seats out of the Hall's total possible capacity of 5,272 remain in private ownership, and these 'seatholders' remain the foundation of the enterprise. The private individuals and corporate seatholders are known as Members of the Corporation. The members contribute to the Hall by paying an annual 'seat rate' and, in order to ensure the financial viability of the Hall, the members have, in addition, foregone their right to attend more than one hundred events each year. The members have acted as as a financial backstop. They have been called upon many times to support the Hall, particularly when the venue was less financially successful than it is now.

The constitution of the Corporation is unique, particularly as its membership is derived from the seatholders. But the setting up, and the governance, of an institution formed in the public interest (and independent of the Government) by means of a Royal Charter is not unusual: most of the national museums, galleries and performing-arts companies – and even the Arts Council itself – were so formed. The Hall's Corporation has a distinct legal

A Royal Vision

The Royal Charter granted by Queen Victoria in 1867 stated that the Hall would be let for eight types of event:

1. National & International Congresses, for the furtherance of the Arts & Sciences
2. Music performances, including those on the organ
3. Distribution of Prizes by Public Bodies & Societies
4. Gatherings of Societies for the promotion of the Arts & Sciences
5. Agricultural and similar Exhibitions
6. National & International Exhibitions of Works of Art & Industries including works by the Artisan classes
7. Exhibitions of Pictures, Sculpture and other objects of artistic or scientific nature
8. Any purposes connected with Science & Art

persona by Act of Parliament and, in acting collectively, its members do so in pursuit of the objects of the Corporation, and with no other purpose.

4. A ROYAL TRIBUTE

On 20 May 1867, a crowd of 7,000 gathered under a temporary marquee, surrounded by rubble, to watch Queen Victoria lay the Hall's red-granite foundation stone. Thousands more lined the route to get a glimpse of the still-grieving monarch, who had rarely been seen in public since her husband's death.

The Queen placed some gold and silver coins and an inscription inside a glass vessel in a cavity underneath the foundation stone, before patting it down with a gold trowel. A twenty-one-gun salute was heard from Hyde Park, and 'Invocation to Harmony', a composition by Prince Albert, was played by an orchestra lead by the celebrated Italian-born conductor Michael Costa.

Queen Victoria then surprised all those present by announcing a change from the Hall's intended name, telling the crowd: 'It is my wish that this Hall should bear his name to whom it will have owed its existence and be called the Royal Albert Hall of Arts and Sciences.'

Queen Victoria later wrote in her diary:

we drove through the Park … up to the place adjoining the Horticultural, where the Hall is to be. It was enclosed and covered in by an enormous tent. Here I got out being received by Bertie [the Prince of Wales, the future Edward VII] … and was conducted to the place where the stone was to be laid … The place was full of people, about 6,000 or more … The National Anthem was sung and then came that most trying moment, from which I suffered severely – the reading of the Address by Bertie and my answer, both full of allusions to my beloved one, which agitated me dreadfully and I was nearly overcome, though I managed to command myself. This over, I went down to the lower platform, only accompanied by our children and those engaged in the laying of the stone. The usual ceremony was gone through … What was very moving and again nearly upset me, was the flourish of trumpets, whilst the stone slowly descended into its place. I then returned to my former place and dearest Albert's composition the *Invocazione all'Armonia* [Invocation to Harmony] was performed … How I thought of dearest Albert's feeling so shy about ever hearing this composition performed, which I had helped in writing down for him, and in singing the solos for him.

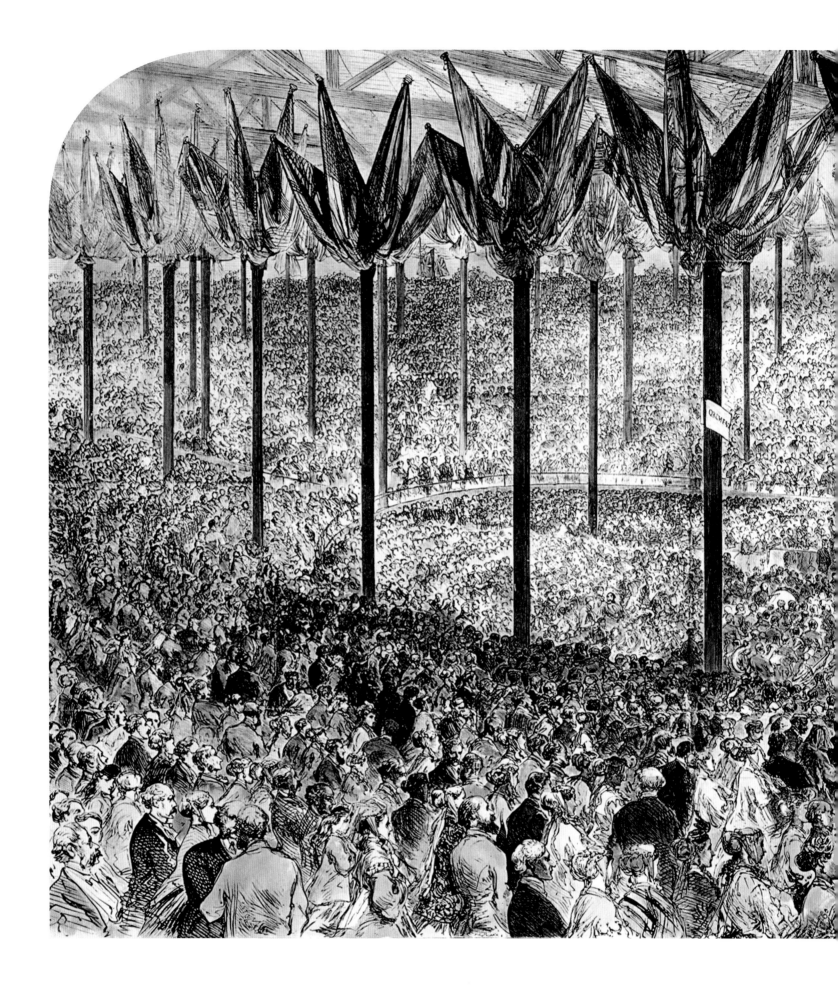

A Royal Vision

LEFT: An illustration of
the official Laying of the
Hall's Foundation Stone
by HM Queen Victoria,
20 May 1867.

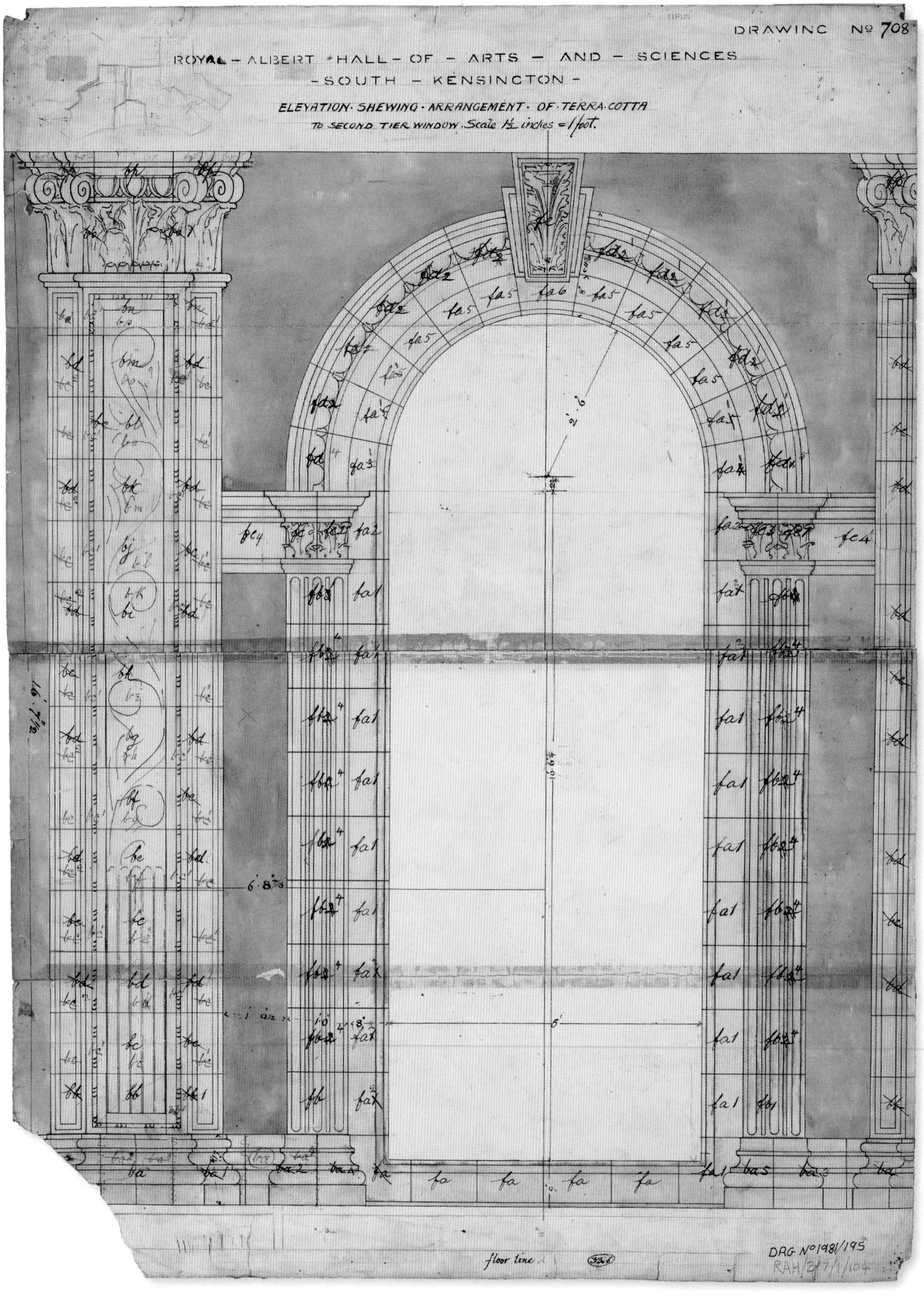

DRAWING Nº 708
ROYAL - ALBERT - HALL - OF - ARTS - AND - SCIENCES
- SOUTH - KENSINGTON -
ELEVATION · SHEWING · ARRANGEMENT · OF · TERRA · COTTA
TO SECOND TIER WINDOW. Scale 1½ inches = 1 foot.
floor line
DRG Nº 1981/195

2 BUILDING & ARCHITECTURE

Visitors to the Hall can't help but be impressed by its intriguing ellipse shape, ornate stone work and magnificent dome. Designed as the perfect concert hall, the auditorium inside was adaptable for all events – stage- based and in the round – and remains so today.

5. A Feat of Engineering

The unique and ingenious design of the Royal Albert Hall is down to two members of the Royal Engineers, Captain Francis Fowke and Major General Henry Scott. Fowke's previous designs included the Royal Museum in Edinburgh, now part of the National Museum of Scotland, and the first major structures built for the South Kensington Museum, which was later renamed the Victoria and Albert Museum. Brought in by Henry Cole, he scaled down the original ambitions for the Hall, coming up with an ornate design that formed the basis for the building that stands today.

Sadly, Fowkes's untimely death in 1865 meant that his colleague, Henry Scott, took over. Although not an architect, Scott was a brilliant innovator who applied his knowledge of engineering and military planning to turning Fowke's sumptuous designs into a practical yet still beautiful building. The architectural challenges of the Hall, Scott said, 'are like strategy; the principles are soon mastered but the difficulty lies in their application, which difficulty is to be overcome by experience.'

Building work began quickly after the laying of the foundation stone, with the first brick laid by Cole's wife, Marian, on 7 November 1867. During the four-year build, 1,620,000 cubic feet (46,000 cubic metres) of earth had to be excavated, while 6,000,000 bricks and 80,000 terracotta blocks were used in the Hall's construction.

The outer wall is an ellipse, 272 feet (83 metres) long and 238 feet (73 metres)

OPPOSITE: Building drawing signed by Henry Young Darracott Scott RE for the construction of the Royal Albert Hall.

Building & Architecture

Dome Truths

The wrought-iron dome weighs 338 tonnes.

The roof glazing weighs 279 tonnes.

The peak of the dome rises 135 feet (41 metres) from the arena floor.

On a cold winter day, it can support 158 tonnes of snow.

In the height of summer, the space between the fluted aluminium ceiling of the auditorium and the glass dome can reach temperatures of up to 64 degrees Celsius.

An interior view of the construction of the dome roof duing the 1870s.

War Office Experiments

The dome played a part in the war effort on 8 June 1918 when War Office agents Edward Heron-Allen and Captain R.W. Legh tested the rate at which copies of a propaganda newspaper, set to be dropped from aircraft over the German lines, would fall by dropping them from the Hall's roof. A diary entry from Heron-Allen explains this 'interesting – and somewhat sensational job':

My part of the work was to go up to the top of the dome and let the papers fall from the lantern on the apex, whilst Legh timed them with a stopwatch on the floor … It is lucky I have 'a head' and do not suffer from vertigo. To get there I had to scale two ladders outside the building – it was easy enough going up, but stepping over the parapet to come down was a moment not to be sought after by anyone who suffers in the least degree from giddiness on a height.

wide, and the auditorium inside measures 103 feet (31 metres) by 68 feet (21 metres). On completion it held 810 seats at floor level. A further 1,642 seats were located in the loggia, grand tier and second tier boxes, while the balcony held 1,783 more. The gallery, which ran around the top of the auditorium, had a standing capacity of 2,000 more people, bringing a total capacity of the Hall when it first opened to 8,285. A corridor wrapped around the entire auditorium led to a promenade of viewing rooms, refreshment rooms, two theatres and offices.

6. Raising the Roof

The most notable of Scott's additions to Fowkes's original plans was the Hall's iconic roof, the largest unsupported dome in the world at the time. Structural engineers Rowland Mason Ordish and John William Grover helped Scott design its 20,000 square feet (1,860 square metres) of wrought iron and glass, with the metal frame being built by the Fairbairn Engineering Company at its factory in Ardwick near Manchester. The frame was then dismantled and brought to London on horse-drawn vehicles and rebuilt, girder by girder, like a huge Meccano set.

Many were afraid the structure would fail, but Scott was determined to prove them wrong. On 11 May 1869, after evacuating the building, he and Grover stood at the top of the scaffolding as the last props were knocked away. Incredibly, the dome dropped just five-sixteenths of an inch (three-quarters of a centimetre) before settling into position on the supporting walls.

During the First World War, London was plunged into darkness by blackouts. The Admiralty ordered that the Royal Albert Hall's dome must be covered, which was achieved with a huge black cloth previously used for film screenings. The dome survived relatively unscathed, losing eight panes of glass when an unexploded anti-aircraft shell hit the south side in 1917. In October 1940, during the Second World War, blasts from three German bombs shattered most of the external windows and destroyed many of the glass panes in the roof; the remaining panes were painted black the following year. Other than that, the Hall was left alone, and German pilots used the distinctive building as a landmark to guide them over London.

7. The Triumph of Arts and Letters

The 800-foot (144-metre) mosaic frieze, which runs around the Hall's outer wall, is a perfect representation of Prince Albert's vision, celebrating both the arts and

Size: 5,200 square feet (483 square metres)

Length: 800 feet (244 metres)

Height: 6 feet 6 inches (2 metres)

Sections: 16

Section Length: 50 feet (15.2 metres)

Artists: 7

Elevation: 84 feet (25.6 metres)

Total cost: £4,426 (equivalent to £416,000 today)

the sciences in pictorial form. Scott's original plan had specified a sculpted frieze but, due to prohibitive costs, the idea of a flat frieze was adopted.

Seven prominent artists were chosen to design the sixteen sections, which celebrate human achievements in music, painting and sculpture, alongside those in astronomy, philosophy, navigation, mechanical engineering, land surveying and architecture. The Great Exhibition of 1851 was represented by Britannia, flanked by female figures of Peace, Concord, Plenty and Prosperity, and with angels at her feet.

Royal Engineer Sergeant Benjamin L. Spackman simulated the final appearance of the sections on the exterior of the Hall by photographing each drawing and then projecting it in 'magic-lantern' style on paper at the correct elevation to help arrive at the frieze's final height of 6 feet 6 inches (two metres), an increase on Scott's original intentions. At this point, the outlines were traced and passed to the tile-making firm of Minton, Hollins & Co., which constructed the curved sections and the tesserae – the pieces were laid entirely by the female students of the mosaic class at the South Kensington Museum. The completed sections were then brought down to the Hall and carried up ladders to be placed in position. Along the top the inscription reads:

THIS HALL WAS ERECTED FOR THE ADVANCEMENT OF THE ARTS AND SCIENCES AND WORKS OF INDUSTRY OF ALL NATIONS IN FULFILMENT OF THE INTENTION OF ALBERT PRINCE CONSORT. THE SITE WAS PURCHASED WITH THE PROCEEDS OF THE GREAT EXHIBITION OF THE YEAR MDCCCLI. THE FIRST STONE OF THE HALL WAS LAID BY HER MAJESTY QUEEN VICTORIA ON THE TWENTIETH DAY OF MAY MDCCCLXVII AND IT WAS OPENED BY HER MAJESTY THE TWENTY NINTH OF MARCH IN THE YEAR MDCCCLXXI. THINE O LORD IS THE GREATNESS AND THE POWER AND THE GLORY AND THE VICTORY AND THE MAJESTY FOR ALL THAT IS IN THE HEAVEN AND IN THE EARTH IS THINE. THE WISE AND THEIR WORKS ARE IN THE HAND OF GOD. GLORY BE TO GOD ON HIGH AND ON EARTH PEACE.

The outer walls of the Hall were also decorated with sixty-three terracotta shields comprised of twenty-five different designs by decorative artist Reuben Townroe. They include the crests of Major General Scott, Queen Victoria, the Prince of Wales and Sir Henry Cole, as well as British national symbols and designs referring to resurrection, mortality and heraldry.

Building & Architecture

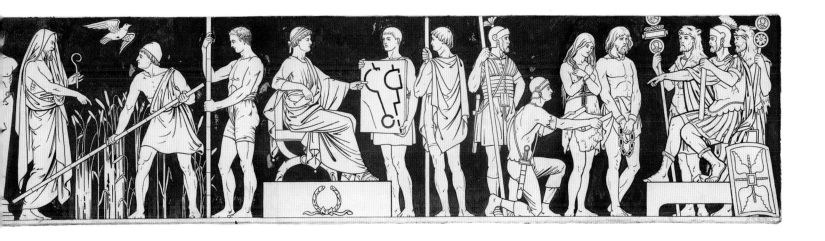

ABOVE AND RIGHT:
The frieze spanning the
circumference of the
Royal Albert Hall.

Building & Architecture

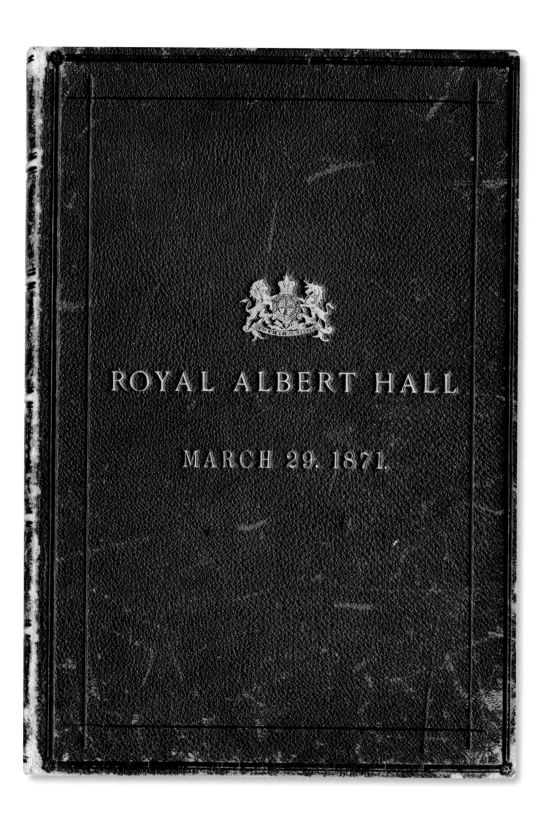

8. The Opening Ceremony

The Royal Albert Hall was opened on 29 March 1871 with a lavish concert attended by Queen Victoria and introduced by the Prince of Wales, later Edward VII, in front of an audience of 8,000.

In his speech, the Prince said that he hoped the Hall would 'contribute to the promotion among my people of the love of art, as well as to the success of the annual exhibitions' that were to display 'the choicest products of the industries of all nations'. In response, the Queen stated: 'I wish to express my great admiration of this beautiful Hall and my earnest wishes for its complete success.' Queen Victoria stayed to listen to Michael Costa's 'A Biblical Cantata', but left before the rendition of her late husband's 'Invocation to Harmony' that followed.

Writing in her diary, she said the crowded hall made her 'quite giddy'. She added: 'Good Mr Cole was quite crying with emotion & delight ... I had never been at such a big function since beloved Albert's time, & it was naturally trying & "émotionnant" for me.'

9. Light and Heat

The pioneering engineering of Fowke and Scott was not limited to the architectural design of the Hall, but was also evident in its lighting, heating and ventilation. Built before the widespread use of electricity, the Hall relied on gas lighting. William Ladd perfected an innovative system that allowed an electric spark, generated by a 'Smee battery' above the inner dome, to ignite 4,210 gas jets in only ten seconds.

On 3 July 1873, just two years after the Hall's opening, the wonders of electricity were put on display in the auditorium for a private visit by Naser al-Din, the Shah of Persia. Electric lighting shone from five points in the gallery using five lamps, each connected to a 'Grove's battery' of 50 cells, placed on the Hall's roof. By 1888, electric lighting had been installed throughout the Hall, including in the boxes. Even after the installation of the electric lights, however, the gas lamps remained as an emergency back-up until they were finally removed in the 1950s. Some of the original pipework can still be found in the building.

Another spectacular innovation was the Hall's ventilation, which consisted of sixty hollow piers – or cylindrical shafts – that were built into the inner walls as both a structural support and an airflow system. Two six-foot (1.8-metre) steam-powered fans, which drew water from a well beneath the Hall, were positioned at either end of the lower part of the system and pumped four million cubic feet (113,000 cubic metres) of air per hour up the hollow centres of the piers and out into the Hall. Today, there are still many removable wall panels on every floor – especially obvious

BELOW: Illustration of the
opening ceremony of the
Royal Albert Hall of Arts
and Sciences, attended by
Queen Victoria, 29 March
1871.

Building & Architecture

behind the pictures on the second tier – which used to house the air 'risers'. They are now used to accommodate electrical cabling and other Hall utilities.

Perforations were also made in the floor to push air up into the arena, which then escaped through an aperture in the domed roof. This air could be cooled with water on hot summer days, or heated by passing through three heating chambers, located under the arena, the stalls and the main corridor. This meant that in winter, a temperature of fourteen to fifteen degrees Celsius could be maintained.

As part of a more recent wider overhaul, a fresh-air ventilation and cooling system, which feeds into the auditorium from under the seats, was introduced between 1996 and 2003. The original ventilation tunnels and shafts were used for ductwork distribution, and a new primary distribution duct was created in a tunnel below the auditorium, supplied from new plant rooms. In 2006, a five-year programme to improve environmental conditions backstage in the upper parts of the auditorium and in the function rooms and bars got underway. In 2013, a programme to replace the thirty-year-old boilers began, and in 2019 both the original boiler house and these later boilers ceased to operate, with more energy-efficient models being installed in their place.

10. A Delicate Matter

There were no toilets inside the Hall when it opened. Instead they were situated in the arcades and conservatory to the south of the building. However, this would not have seemed unusual to Victorian visitors, many of whom would have had no inside bathroom at home. Although the arcades were demolished between 1889 and 1891, the toilets are thought to have stayed outside for a few years. By 1920, they had been moved inside the Hall.

11. A Hall for the Twenty-First Century

Between 1996 and 2004, the Hall underwent a £70-million modernisation, funded by donors private and public donors, including the Heritage Lottery Fund, so that it would be better equipped for the demands of the new century. Incredibly, thirty renovation projects were carried out with minimal disruption to the events programme, with several new bars and restaurants added, better technical facilities, and improvements to the backstage area, including furnished dressing rooms at stage level and principal dressing rooms next to the stage.

Over four weeks in 1996, the circle was rebuilt to add leg room, improve access and enhance sight lines. The stalls were rebuilt over a similar period in 2000, allowing more space underneath for two new bars, while introducing 1,534 specially designed pivoting seats. The largest project was the excavation of the south steps to create a new subterranean loading bay, additional back-of-house offices and dressing rooms, and a residents' car park. Above street level, a new south porch was built, allowing a new cafe bar, box office and retail space to be open to the public throughout the day, as well as during the evening. In addition, the creation of an expansive loading bay enabled the Hall to put on significantly more events, with minimal disruption to surrounding residents and institutions.

BELOW: Graffiti was
displayed in the Hall's
loading bay for the LOAD
Exhibition in June 2009.

During these renovations, the south steps had to be demolished – in the course of the building work, 1,400,000 cubic feet (40,000 cubic metres) of earth were excavated, and 424,000 cubic feet (12,000 cubic metres) of concrete were poured. The total depth of these excavations was 335 feet (18 metres), or the height of five double-decker buses, allowing for the construction of a loading bay wide enough for three lorries to drive in, as well as plant rooms, workshops and service areas in two further levels below.

The new loading bay, which is decorated with commissioned graffiti works from eight talented street artists, can be used as a special performance space and has seen some lively and innovative shows in the last decade. In 2012, it was the venue for a chessboxing tournament, in which competitors alternate a

few minutes of chess with a round of boxing, winning either via a checkmate, a knockout or the referee stopping the contest. For the National Poetry Slam finals in 2014, Steve Larkin was commissioned to write a poem on the history of the Hall, while a couple of silent discos have proved particularly popular with party-goers and neighbours alike.

During their annual visit to the Hall's Festival of Remembrance in 2013, the Queen and Duke of Edinburgh walked out onto the south steps, which had been painstakingly recreated, to view a new paving stone that had been engraved to mark the renaming of the steps as the Queen Elizabeth II Diamond Jubilee Steps, in honour of the previous year's celebrations of the sixtieth anniversary of her accession.

3 ORGAN & ACOUSTICS

Today, every seat in the Hall enjoys the same superior quality of sound, thanks to a state-of-the-art speaker system installed in 2019. But this has not always been the case. Even before the Hall opened its doors in 1871, the architect Henry Scott had identified problems with the acoustics and, over the next century, numerous attempts would be made to fix them.

12. A TROUBLESOME ECHO

Shortly before the opening ceremony, Scott noted, 'Echoes in the Hall very curious', and he was not alone in that opinion. *The Times* report on the historic opening declared that, 'The address was slowly and distinctly read by His Royal Highness [the Prince of Wales], but the reading was somewhat marred by an echo which seemed to be suddenly awoke from the organ or picture gallery, and repeated the words with a mocking emphasis which, at another time, would have been amusing.' In an attempt to fix the problem, a large velarium, or awning, made from sailcloth was hung beneath the dome, which was intended to 'bound the recalcitrant echo in a transparent web', but this did little to alleviate the problem. Investigations revealed a six-second reverberation in some areas and acoustic blind spots in others.

13. WIRED FOR SOUND

In 1894, another experiment saw wires stretched across the auditorium from the gallery columns, each fitted with a length of rabbit netting. The Council's report claimed that the Hall's honorary stewards and seasoned concert-goers 'unanimously' agreed that the wires 'have proved effective in diminishing to a marked degree if not altogether getting rid of the echo.'

In 1924, for a production of Samuel Coleridge-Taylor's *The Song of Hiawatha,*

OPPOSITE: Installation of the iconic acoustic sound diffusers, or 'mushrooms', in 1969.

BELOW: A large scale-shot
of the 135 'mushrooms' lit
up in the Hall.

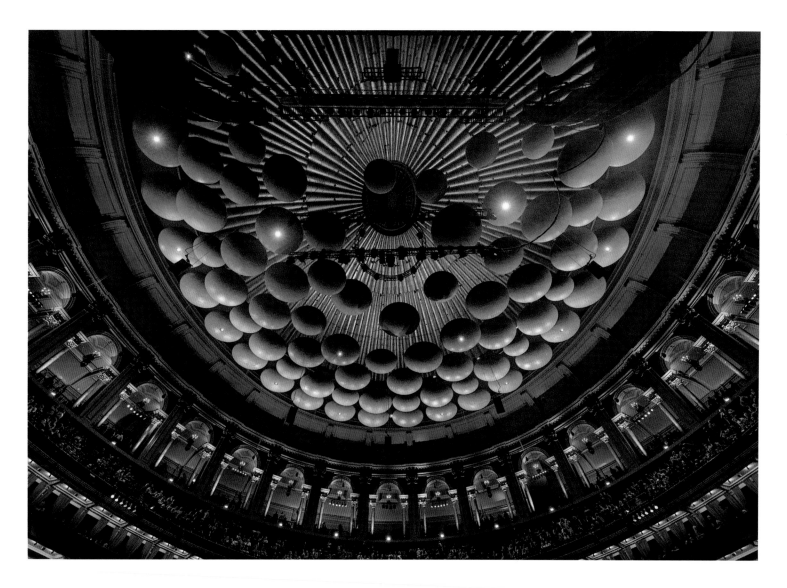

a backcloth measuring 10,000 square feet (930 square metres) and weighing
hundreds of pounds was put up behind the stage. To everyone's surprise and
delight, the huge material was found to improve the acoustics dramatically. Over
the next five years, various plans to install huge swathes of material, including felt
made with asbestos, were mooted and rejected on cost grounds, with one report
estimating that what was needed 'appears to amount to a staggering 45,000 square
feet (4,180 square metres) of felt, costing around £5,000 plus ropes, pulleys and
fixing making around £6,000.' That amounts to around £270,000 in today's
money.

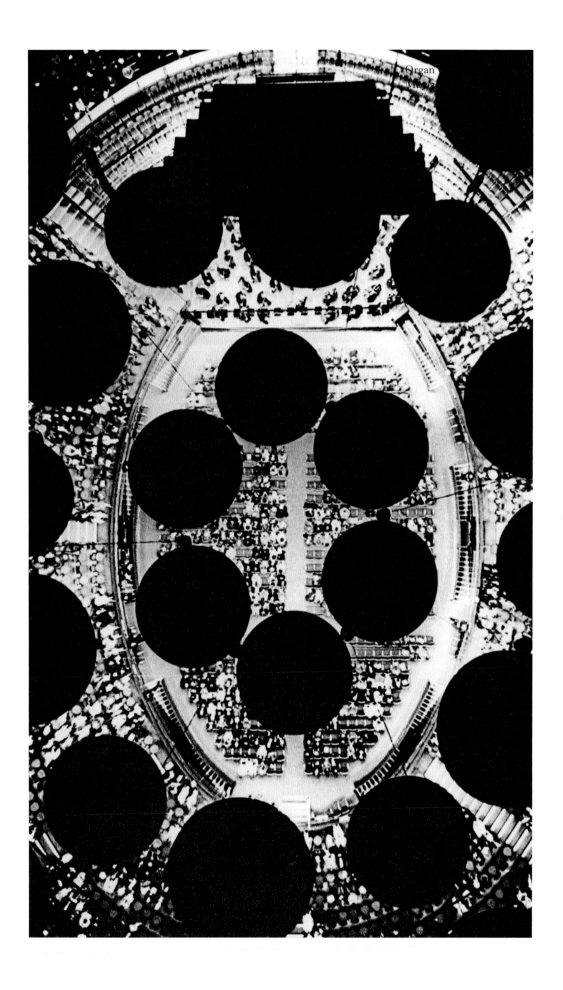

RIGHT: The saucers created a sound canopy that greatly improved acoustics in the Hall.

OVERLEAF: The Grand Organ Celebration, 15 May 2018.

BELOW: The Olivier
Awards at the Royal
Albert Hall on 7 April
2019, where the new audio
system had its debut.

RIGHT: Organ testers
at work before the
inauguration concert after
the six-year refurbishment
of the iconic organ, 20
January 1934.

14. PROMS PROMPT A CHANGE

On the transfer of the famous annual season of concerts, the Proms, to the Hall in 1941, the newly arrived Royal Philharmonic Orchestra brought in some changes of its own having noticed that the acoustics were improved during the Chelsea Arts Club Ball, when the stage was raised. The floors were polished and flags and streamers were draped around the hall, then twenty-foot (six-metre) screens were installed in zigzags around the orchestra, parquet flooring was added behind the conductor, and curtains were placed around the Hall. In addition, a two-tonne, forty-foot- (twelve-metre-) wide sound reflector was hung over the stage.

Eight years later, the velarium and an inner glass dome that had been erected

Sound Saucer-y

135 saucers were installed over two stages in 1969.

The fibreglass mushrooms measure between 6 feet (1.8 metres) and 12 feet (3.7 metres) each.

The largest weighs just 80 pounds (36 kilograms).

There are now just 85 mushrooms, following improvements in 2001.

LEFT: The Grand Organ Celebration on 15 May 2017.

were removed and replaced by the present perforated and fluted aluminium canopy with a Rockwool backing, designed to absorb the sound. However, the improvement to the sound quality proved to be limited.

15. MAGIC MUSHROOMS

A new survey, commissioned in 1968 and led by sound engineer Kenneth Shearer, found that the Hall's echo was caused by the cove in the ceiling. Various tests were conducted, including one that involved an acoustic technician using a reflector microphone while another fired a starting pistol and another played the bassoon. The installation of a series of fibreglass saucers to diffuse the sound was accepted as the best solution.

Fitting these saucers cost £16,000 (£230,000 today), and was carried out in two phases. The first one hundred diffusers, made by the Yorkshire Fibreglass Company, were in place by January 1969 when the BBC Symphony Orchestra, conducted by Colin Davies, held a special test concert. By July that year, all 135 diffusers – now known as 'mushrooms' – were in position for the first night of the Proms, along with a new canopy. William Glock, the man responsible for transforming the Proms into an international festival, was able to write in that year's guide: 'The acoustics have been transformed. The famous echo has become past history.'

16. SURROUND SOUND

Despite the 'mushroom' overhaul, reverberation continued to be an issue and, in 2017, it was decided that new technology could be the answer. Using a 3D projection-mapping model, Sandy Brown Associates ran a series of tests to determine where and why the echo was at its worst, before designing a £2 million speaker system that would finally provide clarity and sound quality for every audience member, as well as reducing the need for touring productions and concerts to install their own equipment.

The new system introduced circle, gallery and box speakers for the first time, bringing the sound closer to all seats. During the six-month project, 465 individual loudspeakers were installed, creating the largest single-room speaker system in the world. To hang the central speakers, twenty-two holes were drilled in the aluminium canopy and twenty-three more were drilled in the plasterwork around the auditorium. Amazingly, as the work was carried out at night, there was no impact on the 327 shows that ran during the upgrade. The new audio system was completed on time and debuted on 7 April 2019 at the prestigious Olivier Awards, which reward excellence at London's theatres.

RIGHT: An extract from *The Suffragette* newspaper detailing the extensive damage to the Hall's organ, July 1914.

from the works of Messrs J. Liversidge & Sons, motor body builders, also in the Old Kent Road. The firemen immediately got to work again. The premises, where a large number of motor-car bodies were stored, were burned to the ground.

Many Thousands of Pounds Damage.

Almost at the same time a fire was reported at Mr Sharp's scenery factory in St. James' Road. These premises also were practically burned out.

Crowds, estimated at 100,000, were attracted by the brilliant glare in the sky. The damage is estimated at many thousands of pounds.

Colonel Fox, Chief of the London Salvage Corps, said to a representative of *The Daily Mail:* "Never in the history of London fires have I known two such big fires raging at the same time within such a short distance."

About 1 a.m. the firemen were trying to keep the flames at Messrs Liversidge's from a large petrol tank and adjacent buildings, including a large paint and varnish works, a cabinetmaker's, a rag factory, and a leather-dressing works.

£2000 DAMAGE AT ALBERT HALL.

Organ Completely Useless.

Under the heading "Suffragette Campaign" the *Daily Telegraph*, June 30, states :—

Another serious outrage of a kind with which the public is now unhappily too familiar occurred in the Albert Hall early on Sunday morning, when the organ was severely damaged by water. At the Clara Butt concert on Sunday afternoon it was noticed that the obbligato to the new song of Sir Edward Elgar was played entirely on the "great" organ, which, as mentioned in the notice of the concert, was not a success, for reasons of intonation and pitch.

It has since been learned that damage to the extent of £2000 has been caused by some person or persons causing the "swell organ" to be flooded with water turned on from the hydraulic tanks.

It is evident that the act was committed by someone to whom the mechanism of the great instrument is familar or to whom, at least, it has been explained. At any rate, the "swell organ" is, it is understood, completely useless, and will be out of action until October, before which time it will be impossible to have it repaired.

ANOTHER OUTBREAK IN NOTTINGHAM.

Nottingham Guardian, June 30.

Papplewick Hall, which is at present untenanted, has been the object of the attentions of the Suffragettes, but their efforts, fortunately, did not meet with success.

Yesterday it was discovered that an entrance had been gained by breaking a window in one of the lower rooms, and firelighters, paraffin, and other inflammable material were placed in such a position as to suit the purpose of rapid firing. Fortunately, the fire, which had been started, had gone out, with the result that beyond the burning of the woodwork no other damage was done.

FIRE AT EDINBURGH TIMBER YARD.

Edinburgh Evening Dispatch, July 6.

About two o'clock on Sunday morning the Edinburgh Fire Brigade received a call to a fire in the woodyard belonging to Messrs F. Walkingshaw & Company, Timber Merchants.

A curious feature of the fire was that while the firemen were at work a strong smell of paraffin oil pervaded the atmosphere, and on examination, two or three bottles which had contained paraffin oil were discovered, while among the timber a clock, saturated with paraffin oil was also found. Quite close to this there was a small handbag filled with saturated cloths. A copy of the SUFFRAGETTE was also found.

The speakers improved levels, tone and clarity for every seat in the room, and ensured that sound quality was consistent throughout the Hall for the first time. 'Regardless of how much you paid for a ticket, you deserve to hear a great performance,' said Steve Jones of D&B Audiotechnik, which fitted the system. 'These changes really democratise the sound.' The Hall's chief executive, Craig Hassall, added that the investment was more than just an improvement in the listening experience of the audience, adding: 'It's about future-proofing the building … so that it is fit for another 150 years.'

17. THE ORGAN

The Hall's famous pipe organ was built by 'Father' Henry Willis, the foremost organ builder of his generation, and completed in 1871. At the time, it was regarded as the largest in the world, standing at 70 feet (21 metres) tall, 65 feet (20 metres) wide, and weighing 150 tonnes. It had four keyboards (known as manuals) and 111 stops; its tin display pipes were 32 feet (9.75 metres) high; and there are 9,999 pipes in total. Many of the exterior pipes, at Henry Cole's suggestion, were visible through three archways in the casework.

The organ was built in Willis's Camden workshop, then assembled over fourteen months in the Hall. Its debut recital was given on 18 July 1871 by William Thomas Best, the Hall's first salaried organist, and a programme of daily recitals followed, attracting audiences of 7,000 people eager to hear 'the voice of Jupiter', as acoustics expert Leo L. Beranek described the instrument in the 1960s.

In July 1914, the organ was damaged by suffragettes, who blocked a sink and left a tap running in a refreshment room next door, which then leaked into the instrument, causing £2,000 worth of damage. The instrument has been through several refurbishments and expansions, first by the firm of Harrison & Harrison between 1924 and 1933, who went on to replace the blowing equipment in the 1950s, and then raised the pitch in the 1960s and updated the electrics in the 1970s. Between 2002 and 2004, it underwent a £1.5 million overhaul by Mander Organs. Due to the extent of all this work, many organ experts now consider the Hall's instrument to be a Harrison & Harrison organ with later Mander improvements, rather than a Father Willis organ. Apart from its case and a few of the pipes, very little of the original organ remains. With its current inventory of 9,999 pipes and 147 stops, the organ is still the second largest in the UK, the largest being the Grand Organ in Liverpool Cathedral, which was completed in 1926 and has 10,268 pipes.

BELOW: Prince Albert,
the chief mouser in the
Hall roaming the organ in
1943.

4 PUTTING ON A SHOW

Over the last 150 years, the number of events on the main stage of the Royal Albert Hall has expanded from twenty-five in 1876 to over 400 a year. As a hall for hire, the venue is open to hosting almost any kind of event – from gala dinners, catwalk shows and sumo wrestling to ice ballets and Cirque du Soleil. No request is too difficult and, providing the production team can adapt the space without damaging the building, anything is considered. Here we look behind the scenes at how the Hall is transformed for spectacular events with the help of its skilled technical team and a whole lot of ingenuity.

The World's Busiest Venue

5,272 capacity in the main auditorium
400 shows in the main auditorium per year

800+ shows in other spaces within the Hall

1,300+ additional events beyond the main stage

1.7 million tickets sold each year

180,000 people inspired through education and outreach

18. MADAM BUTTERFLY

For the 1998 production of Giacomo Puccini's opera *Madam Butterfly*, which centres on the tragic tale of a US serviceman and his young Japanese bride, the arena was flooded to transform it into an enchanting water garden. The set, designed by David Rogers, was based on the residence of a real-life Nagasaki geisha community from the end of the nineteenth century. According to Rogers, 'They lived in a place they called the "floating world" with little islands and bridges to walk over. They lived between the real world and a fantasy world, and that's what they fulfilled for the people who visited them.'

To create the spectacular set, the arena was flooded with 11,000 gallons (50,000 litres) of water, which was then drained for the second half, transforming the space into an austere wasteland. The water was pumped from huge tanks under the stage, as William Elliot from the special-effects company Water Sculptures explains: 'We have eight pumps downstairs and four pumps upstairs to deliver those quantities of water up and down. It takes about fifteen minutes to move

the water up and, in the interval, twelve minutes to remove the water. It just sits under the stage, we filter it, we look after it and we operate it from down there.'

The production returned five times between 2000 and 2015, and Rogers is convinced that the Hall is the only venue where it could be staged. 'There's not a theatre building in Britain that is as powerfully built as the Albert Hall,' he says. 'It's designed to be multipurpose – for circuses, horse races and any event. Another theatre couldn't take the weight of the water. The stage would collapse.'

19. DANCING ON ICE

Although the Hall has been transformed into an ice rink many times, the first time the entire arena was frozen over was for John Curry's *Symphony on Ice* event in April 1984, staged by legendary promotors Victor and Lilian Hochhauser. The Olympic gold medallist – sometimes known as 'the Nureyev of the ice' – led his company of skaters from the United States and Canada for this spectacular ice dance show, accompanied by the Royal Philharmonic Orchestra. 'That was one of the great things that we did at the Albert Hall,' recalled Victor Hochhauser. 'John Curry was one of the greatest dancers ever – he was definitely ballet on ice.' The

OPPOSITE: The John
Curry Skating Company's
production of *A Symphony
on Ice*, 8 April 1984.

RIGHT AND OVERLEAF:
The Imperial Ice Stars
performing *Cinderalla
on Ice* at the Hall, 28
February 2010.

Putting on a Show

16,000 square feet (1,486 square metres) – area of the floor

1,300 – maximum number of diners at a dinner dance

2,000 – maximum number of guests at a dance

8 square feet (0.75 square metres) per dancer

30 workers take thirteen and a half hours to lay the floor.

1,500 chairs covering the floor of the arena are removed

7 feet 2 inches (2.2 metres) – height of the Exhibition Floor above the arena's floor

1.25 miles (2 kilometres) of solid beams are laid

350 sheets of plywood are then placed over the top

2,000 screws fasten the wood

Opposite: Charles Cochran (Manager of the Royal Albert Hall) with Mr Birch (Clerk of Works) inspecting the new Great Floor, 1936.

show went swimmingly, despite early concerns before the first performance. At the end of the run, the ice was chopped up, put in skips and then dumped in the River Thames.

Amazingly, the first skating rink in the Hall was constructed as early as March 1889, for an ice carnival, bazaar and festival held for the benefit of the West End Hospital, which featured snowshoe races and comic skaters. Other ice shows have included David Essex's *Beauty and The Beast* in 1995, at which an extended stage formed the rink. During one performance, Essex was surprised by *This is Your Life* host Michael Aspel, who ambushed him with the famous red book.

Transforming the Hall into an ice rink takes up to forty-eight hours. In February 2010, when the Imperial Ice Stars staged *Cinderella on Ice*, an artificial pond was created on the arena floor and nine tonnes of crushed ice were evenly spread around before being sprayed with water. The ice was kept frozen by sixteen miles (twenty-six kilometres) of piping connected to three chillers in the basement.

20. Making Space

For some events, such as tennis matches, motor shows and banquets, more floor space is required in the auditorium, but that problem was solved early on by our Victorian predecessors. In the 1880s, the Hall's Council approved the building of the 'Great Floor', a 16,800-square-foot (1,560-square-metre) wooden platform that could be installed as required to bring the whole arena up fifteen feet (four and a half metres), reaching the level of the lower parts of the loggia boxes. The Great Floor was supported by hundreds of foot-thick wooden posts, each bolted into position by a complex system of rods and ties. The floor broke down into several sections, with each segment and support numbered for easy assembly. Unfortunately, the Great Floor's introduction meant that the seatholders had to relinquish their seats during events for which it was needed but most were willing to make the sacrifice. One pair of particularly stubborn sisters, the Misses Mirchhouse, were not so accommodating, demanding a hole be cut in the floor so they could still take their seats during a ball. Whether they sat unmoved while dancers whirled around them has sadly not been recorded.

After the first event to use the new structure – the Charing Cross Bazaar of 1889 – the floor was dismantled and stored in the vaults and, the Council decreed, 'was found to be satisfactory in every way'. Subsequent events that used the Great Floor included car shows in the 1930s, most frequently those mounted by Ford, and the notorious Chelsea Arts Club Balls. In 1936, a new floor supported by tubular-steel pillars and rolled-steel joists was purchased and used until the

Putting on a Show

mid-1980s. Its hardwood floorboards could be sprung for dancing or left rigid, and their resilience was tested by driving cars across the surface at 'as great a speed as skidding on the smooth surface' would allow. Designed by Francis W. Troup, the new floor could be constructed in twenty-four hours.

This second floor was replaced in 1991 by an aluminium substructure that could be placed over the stalls, raising the whole arena to cover the first five rows of the stalls. The new 'Exhibition Floor', topped with marine plywood, cost £250,000 and was designed to maximise the Hall's commercial potential, providing a greater space for dinners and dances. The floor is built in sections and takes one day either side of an event to install and dismantle. The Exhibition Floor is now used for many events, including large dinners and the annual Champions Tennis tournament.

21. CAR TROUBLE

The growing popularity of cars in the 1930s led to a rise in motor shows, and in 1932, the Hall hosted its first Ford Motor Exhibition. On top of the logistical issues involved in getting several cars into the auditorium, the Hall faced the

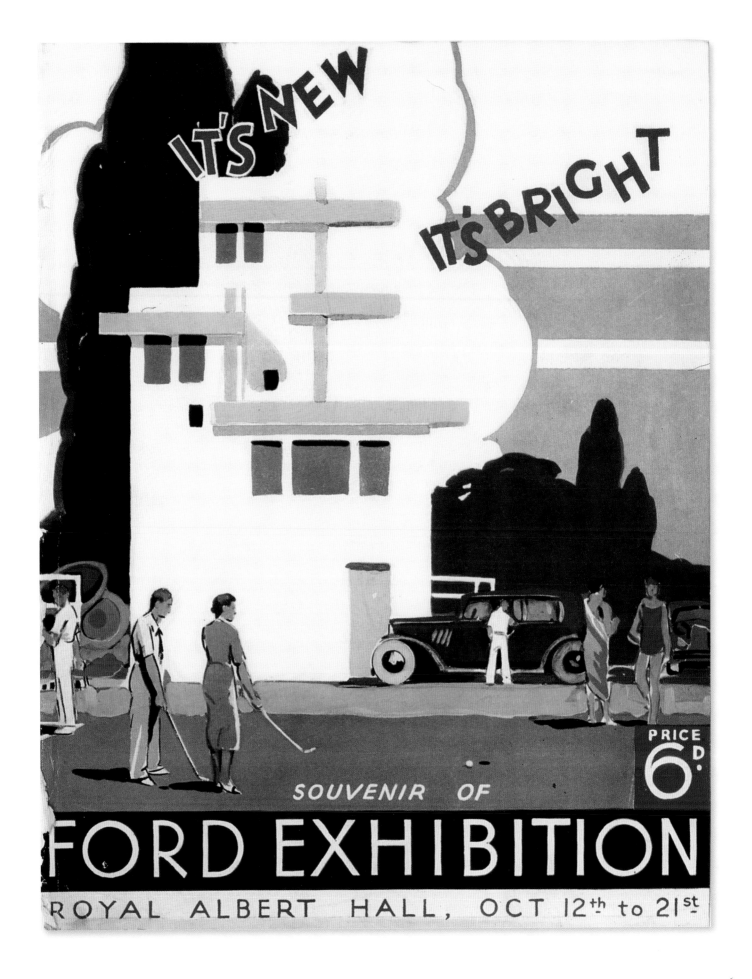

In order to lift the heavy lighting, props and motors that need to be suspended from the domed roof for many shows, a system of motorised chain hoists is in place:

The rigging system consists of 100 permanently rigged chain hoists.

The hoists travel at a fixed speed of 13 feet (4 metres) per minute.

The distance from the arena floor to the corona is 150 feet (45 metres), so it can take around ten minutes to lift some equipment into position.

If a chain hoist is required to lift two tonnes, double the amount of chain is required – 300 feet (90 metres) in total – and, combined with the body of the motor, each hoist weighs around 265 pounds (120 kilograms).

challenge presented by Ford's desire to display a number of large, heavy tractors in the gallery. The problem was solved by removing the framework of some large street doors, then using ramps to push the vehicles up the stairs, across the corridor around the outside of the auditorium, and on to the Great Floor. Having been pushed in, the tractors were then hauled into position from the floor using ropes and pulleys. The Motor Exhibition ran for a fortnight, annually, for five years – the boxes acted as sales offices and films showcasing Ford's latest models were screened in the West Theatre, known today as the Elgar Room.

The auction house Christie's has also held car sales in the Hall over the years, but without using the Great Floor, thus the cars had to be pushed down ramps through the stalls onto the arena floor and stage. At one such auction in 1987, ten of the rarest vintage cars were sold, including a 1931 Bugatti Royale Kellner Coupe (one of only six ever made), two Rolls-Royces from 1911 and 1928, and a 1926 Mercedes built for the Austrian opera singer Richard Tauber. Luckily, these precious vehicles made it in and out of the Hall without a scratch.

22. HEAVY LIFTING

The original plans for the building included two lifts and, while two shafts were built, only one was used. Located on the west side of the Hall, this housed London's first hydraulic lift, built using a ramrod made of polished steel in sections seventy inches (178 centimetres) long. A corresponding shaft on the east side sat empty, and both of these original shafts were filled in 1900 when two new lifts were installed. In addition, in the 1930s a staircase was partially demolished to accommodate a larger lift.

Today the Hall has eight lifts, including three public lifts and a catering lift. The arena is served by three lifts, all powered from a panel in the basement underneath, and operated by remote control. 'These lifts, added in the refurbishment in the late 1990s, are a critical addition to the building,' says Ollie Jeffery, head of production and technical at the Hall. 'They are one of the main reasons we are able to do such a huge variety of shows that we may not have been able to do before.'

23. THE CIRCUS COMES TO TOWN

One of the most complex and labour-intensive transformations is for the annual residence of Cirque du Soleil – the acrobatic troupe has undertaken an extended run at the Hall every year since 1996, apart from two years during the redevelopments. Each year the death-defying stunts require new props, from

BELOW: Cirque du Soleil's
Luzia at the Royal Albert
Hall, 6 February 2020.

RIGHT: A Cirque du
Soleil performer defies
gravity during their show
OVO, 18 January 2018.

Maintenance Week

With footfall that runs into thousands every day, the Hall needs a regular spruce-up so, twice a year, the doors close for maintenance week. The technical team need a head for heights as the 'corona', the central part of the circular roof, has to be inspected, with staff standing on its steel-wire tension grid 150 feet (45 metres) above the floor. Other members of the team are winched up to the ceiling to inspect and clean every one of the eighty-five acoustic mushrooms.

Crucial stage equipment, such as the chain hoists in the roof, are all checked and serviced. The famous red walls and box fronts in the arena get a fresh lick of paint, and upholstery is checked and revamped where necessary. The floor is relaid to make sure it can withstand another six months of excited audiences and incredible shows in the round.

the impressively high trees in a production entitled Varekai, which stood 34 feet (10.3 metres) tall, to a 1,600-pound (726-kilogram) wheel of death in Kooza. In 2020, for the production of Luzia, a constant stream of water cascading from the heavens meant that huge water tanks had to be installed in the Hall.

'Cirque bring everything themselves and there are some really big challenges,' says Jeffery. 'So in 2020, with the rainfall effect, we had to look at where we put the water tanks, how we installed the plumbing, how we got the water pressure right. In any other building, Cirque just build a tank but they are coming into a Grade I listed building, and different rules apply.'

In recent years, the Hall's Christmas ballet – *The Nutcracker* by Pyotr Illyich Tchaikovsky – has wrapped up on New Year's Eve, and the loading for Cirque will begin the next day at six o'clock in the evening. The build can take up to twelve days, with around one hundred workers, and between thirty and forty trucks will arrive in the loading bay during that time. In fact, work will have already been underway for two weeks by that point, with teams working overnight rigging motors in the roof void and checking anchor points with the Hall's structural engineers.

A scaffolding grid and 25-foot (7.6-metre) revolving ring are constructed on the arena floor before being winched to the ceiling. Lighting clusters are then hung from the ring, as are anchor points for the aerial-acrobatics apparatus. The winch in the centre of the carousel can lift up to 990 pounds (450 kilograms) at ten feet (three metres) per second.

It's not just the auditorium and the dressing rooms that the circus troupe commandeers during its long stay. The gallery is usually available for hire for dinner and drinks before and during shows, but during the Cirque's residence it becomes a gym for the ultra-fit performers, with exercise bikes, running machines and weight-lifting equipment taking up the scenic space. Looking back on the Cirque du Soleil's arrival in 1996, the Hall's former financial director Peter Jervis recalls:

It was a real game-changer because, prior to that, January had been notoriously difficult to fill, and now there were thirty-two or more shows. It took everyone by surprise because Cirque du Soleil was a pretty unknown quantity in the UK. After the first night, the reviews came out and they were astonishing. Then it just went crazy. People couldn't buy tickets fast enough and because they were buying them at very short notice it meant most of them had to be picked up at the venue. The box office had to put a call-out to the entire staff saying, 'You've got to come down and help us because we can't give the tickets out quick enough!' Everyone

RIGHT: Backstage at Birmingham Royal Ballet's *The Nutcracker*.

OVERLEAF: Dancers from the Birmingham Royal Ballet during a production of *The Nutcracker*, 29 December 2017.

Putting on a Show

from finance, sales and building development was down in the box office just chucking out tickets. It was an astonishing success story, and it's still going now.

24. The Phantom of the Opera

It is not unusual for a production build to take longer than the run of a show. For example, the twenty-fifth anniversary of Andrew Lloyd Webber's *The Phantom of the Opera*, presented by Cameron Mackintosh in October 2011, had just three performances over two days, but the build had the whole production team working flat out for five days. The lavish production was beamed into cinemas around the country, and starred Ramin Karimloo as the Phantom and Sierra Boggess as Christine. They were joined by a cast and orchestra of over 200, together with some special guest appearances.

'One of the great strengths of *The Phantom of the Opera* is that, being set in an opera house, its production is totally theatrical,' said Cameron Mackintosh. 'We felt that there could be no better nineteenth-century theatrical auditorium in London for this occasion than the Royal Albert Hall. With its Victorian red plush and its celebrated magnificent organ, it is the perfect place for the Phantom to haunt.'

The Royal Albert Hall was transformed into the show's opera house by integrating the set with the existing boxes, extending the decorative plasterwork all the way round the auditorium. The sumptuous set also included a huge glass chandelier which, with the rigging needed to lift it, weighed 2,650 pounds (1,200 kilograms), and required approximately 170 chain hoists to get it into place. When the final curtain fell, the team had just six hours to bring the set down in preparation for the next production.

25. The Nutcracker

The length of time it takes to prepare the Hall for a show varies wildly from four or five hours to over a week. A straight orchestral show, for example, will begin loading in at seven o'clock in the morning and will be ready for rehearsals by half past two in the afternoon. If a show finishes at ten o'clock at night, the set will be loaded out until seven o'clock the following day. However, for a more sophisticated build such as an Eric Clapton show, the load can start as early as three o'clock in the morning, to finish by one o'clock in the afternoon.

One of the biggest builds each year is *The Nutcracker*, which runs between Christmas and New Year. Brought to life by Birmingham Royal Ballet, Tchaikovsky's classic ballet centres on the night before Christmas, when the toys in the Victorian home of the young heroine Clara come to life and dance. The production features a Christmas tree that grows on stage, after which comes 'the magical moment it snows in front of the awestruck audience', as the *Daily Express* put it.

The *Nutcracker* is a massive build, requiring a huge raised orchestral platform at the back of the stage and a set constructed by the Royal Opera House at their warehouse in Thurrock. Mirrors along the front of the platform change for the different scenes, and when the Christmas tree appears on stage, screens come up from the choirs and slowly lift as the tree gets bigger and bigger.

Nutcracking Facts

The show features:

165 pounds (75 kilograms) of artificial snow

An on-stage cast of some 60 dancers

Over 200 stunning period costumes

Over 45 wigs and pieces of facial hair

The King Rat costume is the heaviest, weighing in at 22 pounds (10 kilograms)

500 hairpins per show – that's a staggering 3,500 hairpins over the run of seven shows

5 STAR TURNS

Throughout its 150-year history, the Royal Albert Hall has played host to thousands of musical headliners, ranging from rock and opera to punk and pop. The stage has been commanded by the all-time greats, including the Beatles, Frank Sinatra and Joan Armatrading, and world-renowned contemporary artists, such as Adele, Emeli Sandé and Kylie Minogue. But, as well as being a celebrated music venue, the Hall has been headlined by a huge range of comedy stars, including Victoria Wood, Monty Python, Russell Brand, John Bishop and Russell Howard.

26. ADELINA PATTI, 1888

Among the first headliners to pack the auditorium with admirers was Adelina Patti. She became an opera superstar in her early teens, performing in 1860 for the Prince of Wales in Montreal at the age of just seventeen. The Spanish-born singer made her debut at the Albert Hall in 1880 at a grand operatic concert, before her performing her first solo show in 1888. At the height of her fame, the formidable diva demanded to be paid $5,000 in gold before each performance. Her contracts stipulated that her name was to be top-billed and printed larger than any other cast member, and that while she was 'free to attend all rehearsals, she was not obligated to attend any'. In his memoirs, opera promoter 'Colonel' James Henry Mapleson revealed Patti, an astute businesswoman, had trained her parrot to squark 'Cash! Cash!' whenever he walked into the room.

Patti played her last professional concert on 1 December 1906, at the Royal Albert Hall, although she returned to the Hall for one last performance, in aid of the Red Cross, in October 1914.

RIGHT: Programme for
Madame Adelina Patti –
Grand Morning Concert,
20 June 1891.

Star Turns

27. DAME NELLIE MELBA, 1898

Operatic soprano Helen Porter Mitchell, better known under her stage name of Madame Nellie Melba, played her first sell-out crowd at the Hall in 1898, twenty years before receiving her damehood. Over the next three decades the Australian star, who took her stage name from her hometown of Melbourne, performed at the Hall a total of twenty-six times, often at the Sunday Concerts, which ran from 1889 to 1950. Her farewell appearance, in 1926, was conducted by Henry Wood – the archives recall that, to mark the occasion, 'a rope was hung across in front of organ with Union Jack in centre and three Australian flags at each side'.

In March 2009, the music critic John Steane wrote of Melba's voice: 'A correspondent who was present at Melba's last concert at the Albert Hall described the sensation of feeling that wherever you were seated in that vast place you could put out a hand and touch it.'

28. GRACIE FIELDS, 1938

The Rochdale-born singer and actress Gracie Fields made her Royal Albert Hall debut on 29 October 1938, at a charity fundraiser for the London Hospital Bicentenary Appeal. Queen Mary, the wife of George V, was watching from the royal box, and Fields admitted that the royal presence caused her 'bother', as she was worried that many of her comedy numbers were 'a little crude', but she told the press afterwards that 'Queen Mary was sweet, perfectly sweet'. Fields also admitted that she had always been too frightened to play the Hall because of the size of the venue, but added she could swallow her nerves for charity. 'When you do something for others you can do for them what you can't do for yourself,' she said. 'When I first came onto the platform I was so scared and I felt so small, I should have liked to have gone onto my knees on the stage.'

Fields' last appearance at the Hall was in 1964, at the private Baird Festival of Television, when she was sixty-six. She appeared alongside Arthur Askey, Ned Sherrin and a young Bruce Forsyth, who was making his Royal Albert Hall debut.

29. ALL THAT JAZZ

Throughout the 1950s, jazz was a huge part of the Royal Albert Hall programme, with events such as the Jazz Cavalcade Star Parade and the All-Night Carnival of Jazz. Stars including Cab Calloway, Sarah Vaughan, Mario Lanza and Ella Fitzgerald played to packed houses and, in 1954, Billie Holiday joined forces

OPPOSITE: Programme
for Billie Holiday with
Jack Parnell and his
Orchestra, 14 February
1954.

with legendary bandleader Jack Parnell and his orchestra for a special concert sponsored by the *New Musical Express*. The American legend wowed the audience with moving renditions of her classic hits, including 'Strange Fruit', 'Lover Man' and 'All of Me'.

30. ROCK 'N' ROLL ROYALTY

The Beatles first played the Hall on 18 April 1963 at a show called Swinging Sounds '63, and were halfway down a bill which boasted Matt Monro, Del Shannon, Susan Maughan, Lance Percival and Shane Fenton and the Fentones. The gig was a huge hit – especially when the Fab Four unexpectedly broke into 'Twist and Shout', getting the whole audience on their feet and twisting the night away.

Later that year, on 15 September, they played their second and final gig at the Hall, this time topping the bill in the Great Pop Prom. Since their first appearance they had soared to number one with 'She Loves You' and launched their own radio series – Beatlemania was in full swing. 'It was the siege of the Beatle-crushers … 6,000 screaming teenagers intent on crushing just four Beatles,' reported the *Daily Mirror*. 'Never has the Royal Albert Hall seen scenes quite like it. Even for Britain's newly elected top vocal group, the Beatles, it was bewildering.'

Another up-and-coming band, the Rolling Stones, were watching the mayhem from the wings, having played their set. It was the first of only a handful of occasions that these giants of rock would appear on the same bill, and a picture to mark the occasion was taken on the south steps. Paul McCartney, quoted in *Alf Bicknell's Beatles Diary*, later recalled, 'Standing up on those steps behind the Albert Hall in our new gear, the smart trousers, the rolled collar. Up there with the Rolling Stones we were thinking, "This is it – London! The Albert Hall!" We felt like gods.' Stones bassist Bill Wyman later recalled: 'We opened the show, and the Beatles watched us. They told us years later that they were very nervous with the reception we got.'

The Beatles were booked to return to the Hall later that year for the New Year's Eve Ball but, after concerns were raised over safety and the potential wear and tear caused by over-ardent fans, they were quietly pulled from the bill. The Fab Four never played the Hall again as a foursome – although John, Paul, George and Ringo all returned individually over the years – but they retain one unforgettable link to the iconic building through the lyrics to the 1967 track 'A Day in the Life'.

"NEW MUSICAL EXPRESS"
LTD.
present (by arrangement with Harold Davison)

BILLIE HOLIDAY

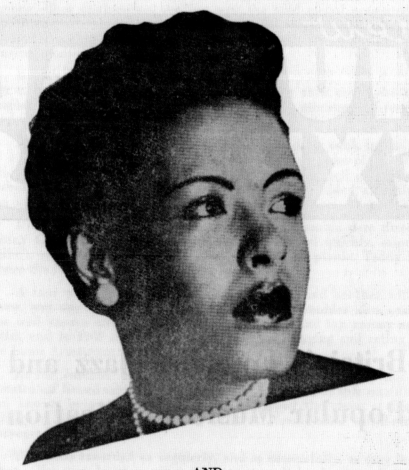

AND

JACK PARNELL & HIS ORCHESTRA

Royal Albert Hall — Sunday, Feb. 14, 1954

Star Turns

OPPOSITE: Programme
for Swinging Sound '63,
18 April 1963.

BELOW: The Beatles
perform at the The
Great Pop Proms, in aid
of the Printers Pension
Corporation,
15 September 1963.

THE ROLLING STONES

On the evening of May 10th, five R 'n B fanatics assembled in a recording studio. The results were: "Come On" and, flipside, "I Wanna Be Loved". The Rolling Stones, formed 11 months ago to dep for a group at The Marquee, London, where they got a wildly enthusiastic reception – had cut their first disc; on May 15th the tapes were played to top Decca executives and a decision was taken to rush release the record on June 7th!

Stone by Stone, here they are :– Mick Jagger, 19 – Lead/Vocal and Harmonica – likes money ; Brian Jones, 19 – Guitar/ Vocals and Harmonica – smokes 60 a day ; Keith Richard, 19 – Guitar – wants a Thames house-boat ; Bill Wyman, 21 – Bass Guitar/Vocals – a Chuck Berry fan, and Charlie Watts – the Beau Brummel of the group – Drums.

We're sure you'll give this madly exciting group the same tumultuous hearing they've already had all over London and the Home Counties !

the BEATLES

The original Beatles group of John, Paul and George exploded into the Merseyside scene in 1960. Having made their impression there, they at once took off on the first of 5 brilliant night club seasons in Hamburg.

They made Pop history last year when joined by Ringo Starr (drums) their debut deck, "Love Me Do", sold enough copies during its first 48 hours in the shops to soar straight into the National Hit Parade. Not only have they since squeezed 2 Number One winners " Please Please Me " and " From Me To You " into their first six months' of recording ; they've scored a fantastic EP success, too, with "Twist and Shout".

I read the news today oh boy

Four thousand holes in Blackburn, Lancashire

And though the holes were rather small

They had to count them all

Now they know how many holes it takes to fill the Albert Hall

31. RECORD BREAKING ROCKER

Guitarist Eric Clapton has played the Royal Albert Hall over 200 times, making him the venue's most prolific living headliner. Since his first performance with the Yardbirds in 1964, 'Slowhand', as he is affectionately known, has appeared alongside the likes of Paul McCartney and Sting in gala performances, and headlined numerous residencies as a solo artist. Two of his most iconic moments were with his early band Cream, whose farewell concert was screened by the BBC on 5 January 1969 as *Omnibus: Cream the Last Concert* – the event has since become known as simply 'Farewell Cream'.

While fans and critics loved the gig, Clapton was not happy with it, admitting that the band were under-rehearsed and he was under the influence of a 'substance'. Almost four decades later, in 2005, Cream played a series of reunion shows over four nights in May to 'set the record straight'. This time the band rehearsed solidly for a month, and Clapton recently recalled:

We were clearly off our heads when we did that first one and by the time we did the reunion we had cleaned up our act. For the Farewell concert we didn't rehearse at all, we hadn't been rehearsing for a long time, we just rolled up and played whatever we liked. There was no structure whatsoever. The thing I remember more than anything else this time was the standing ovation that wouldn't stop. We didn't know what to do because they wouldn't sit down. For me that was the best Cream gig of all, and it had to be in the Albert Hall. What we did in the Albert Hall was for the love of it. It wasn't for the money but to try and restore something we thought we had lost. It was to say goodbye, again, but in a way we could remember with good emotion.

Between 1987 and 1996, Clapton performed annual winter residencies as a solo artist, peaking in 1991 with twenty-four shows with four different band line-ups, including a full orchestra. 'It's a bit like Wimbledon,' he said of his yearly shows. 'As long as I could do it I would do it.' Even after the annual shows stopped, Clapton returned on a regular basis for both his solo shows and charity benefits.

A Mural of Stars

Prominent British artist Peter Blake has had a long relationship with the Royal Albert Hall. He first attended in the 1940s, coming to Prom concerts with his family. He graduated from the Royal College of Art at the Hall, watched wrestling matches and rock concerts, and even held his eightieth birthday in the gallery. As the man who created the iconic album cover for the Beatles' *Sgt. Pepper's Lonely Hearts Club Band*, with its famous reference to the Hall, he was the obvious choice when it came to creating a mural of the many headliners who had starred at the venue over the years.

The resulting 10-foot- (3-metre-) wide artwork, *Appearing at the Royal Albert Hall*, was unveiled at the Royal Albert Hall in April 2014, and can be seen in the Zvi and Ofra Meitar Porch and Foyer. It is a montage of more than 400 stars who have appeared since 1871, including music legends such as Bob Dylan, David Bowie and Jimi Hendrix – and of course the Beatles – to major figures in the arts and sciences such as Albert Einstein, Stephen Hawking and J. K. Rowling.

'I was honoured when the Royal Albert Hall commissioned me to create this mural,' said Blake. 'The project instantly captured my imagination – the ultimate opportunity to promote the arts in one of Britain's greatest venues, combined with the challenging process of immortalising over 400 of the world's most popular artists.'

ABOVE: Peter Blake Mural
at the Royal Albert Hall.

RIGHT: Eric Clapton celebrates his 100th performance at the Royal Albert Hall in 1994.

Star Turns

Russell Howard – Most performances on consecutive nights, with ten nights in 2017

Victoria Wood – Longest run by a comedian, with fifteen shows, in both 1993 and 1996

Eric Clapton – Hall's most prolific headliner, with over 200 concerts

Charles Aznavour – Oldest headliner at the age of 91, in 2015

World's Biggest Samba Band – 1,500 schoolchildren from twenty-seven London schools in 2015

Largest Kazoo Ensemble – 3,910 kazooists for Red Nose Day in 2011

Largest Ocarina Ensemble – 3,081 children and audience members played the small wind instrument in 2013

Largest Knitting Circle – 3,083 members of the Women's Institute broke the record for the number of people knitting together in 2012

As of May 2019, he had graced the stage 211 times, and the Hall remains his favourite venue:

> The Albert Hall is probably one of the only venues where you're not looking out at a black hole which is why I like it, because you can see your friends in the second row of the stalls. It's like being in someone's living room, it's such an intimate place to play or to see someone else play.

In 2018, Clapton's part in the Hall's history was honoured when he became one of eleven inaugural recipients of the Royal Albert Hall Star. His star can be seen outside the venue, between door twelve and the stage door.

32. ELECTRIC STORM

In May 1965, Bob Dylan made his debut at the Hall, ending his last ever acoustic tour with two dates. When he returned a year later, he played the second half of the concert with the backing of an electric band – to the horror of many of his diehard fans. 'There was a marked and disturbing contrast between the two parts of the concert given by Bob Dylan, the American folk singer, at the Albert Hall last night,' reported *The Times*. 'In the first, and infinitely better, half of the evening, Mr Dylan gave an agreeable solo rendering of some of the songs for which he is best known: in the second half he was accompanied by the thunderous quintet who made it virtually impossible to distinguish a single line of the lyrics.'

Bizarrely, the now legendary Dylan bootleg entitled *Live at the Albert Hall* was actually recorded in the Manchester Free Trade Hall on the same tour, but the strength of feeling over his switch to electric sound can be heard on the record, with one audience member shouting 'Judas!' Another man shouted, 'I'm never listening to you again,' to which Dylan famously responded, 'I don't believe you, you're a liar.'

After an absence of forty-seven years, Dylan returned to a calmer Royal Albert Hall for three dates in 2013, and was met with a rapturous reception. In 2015, he marked the fiftieth anniversary of his first appearance with five sold-out gigs. A five-star review from the *Evening Standard* enthused, 'On this form, he's a privilege to watch. This was a legend being legendary.'

33. EUROVISION IN COLOUR, 1968

The thirteenth edition of the annual Eurovision Song Contest took place at the Hall on 6 April 1968, following Sandie Shaw's win at the previous year's event

BOB DYLAN has systematically shaken, upset, overturned and finally re-routed the entire course of contemporary folk music. There isn't a singer in the folk field today who hasn't in some way been influenced by him, in his writing, his performing, even in his appearance. The imitators are legion, but Dylan continues on his own way, belonging to no-one, blazing his own trails — exciting, unpredictable, unexcelled.

ABOVE: Programme for
Bob Dylan's show, 26-27
May 1966.

The seatholder Larry Viner recalled his memories of Bob Dylan's 1965 concert at the Hall:

'I was a young man who was besotted with Bob Dylan, and the first half was magic. In the second half they plugged in the electric guitars and I was traumatised. I shouted out "Judas!" Shortly after the concert they brought out a bootleg album, Live at the Albert Hall. *You could hear me shouting out "Judas!" I'd made rock 'n' roll history, or so I thought. Over the subsequent years, if ever the conversation came up about the Bob Dylan bootleg and the "Judas!" shout, I proudly told them that it was me. In fact, I met Bob Geldof many years later, who shook my hand and said, "That was wonderful." Many years later, they did some special programmes on Bob Dylan at the Albert Hall and that famous shout, and to my horror they were talking to a man in Manchester, who claimed it was him on the recording. He was correct. The bootleg of* Live at the Albert Hall *was misnamed. It turned out that throughout the tour everyone was shouting "Judas!", so I was just one of many. I went from rock 'n' roll hero to rock 'n' roll zero.'*

Star Turns

with 'Puppet on a String'. Hosted by Katie Boyle, the event was televised in colour for the first time in the UK, as well as being shown in France, Germany, the Netherlands, Norway, Switzerland and Sweden. Despite being favourite to win, the UK entry – 'Congratulations' by Cliff Richard – was pipped to the post by the Spanish singer Massiel, whose song 'La La La' got one vote more. In 2008, a Spanish journalist alleged that the vote had been rigged by the dictator Francisco Franco, who had bribed television executives and record companies across Europe, but this allegation was later dropped when an outraged Massiel pointed out that, given her political affiliations, 'other singers, who were more keen on Francoist Spain, would have benefitted' if the claim had been true.

34. Janis Joplin's Only Solo Gig
Folk singer Janis Joplin was at the forefront of the 1960s counterculture movement, and was met with a rapturous reception when she played her only

solo gig in London, at the Royal Albert Hall on 21 April 1969. *The Daily Telegraph* described it as one of the most 'electrifying "happenings" of the counterculture era', saying, 'Forget all you may have read or heard … Here in fact was the comfortingly embodied voice of love, pain, yearning, freedom and ecstatic experience, a fire that speaks from the heart of warm, rounded flesh.' Other reviews noted that the singer turned the Hall into a 'discoteque with her invitation to dance', and that 'her hour of belting, grinding vocalising against her soul-slanted backing group had created enough excitement and emotion to make the audience forget their inhibitions … They responded by dancing in the aisles, the boxes, and on the stage'

The *New Musical Express* had backstage access and reported:

[Joplin] bursts into the green room of the Royal Albert Hall like the cork from a bottle of Moet et Chandon champagne. Excited, elated and bubbling over Janis Joplin couldn't have been happier. 'We did it, we did it!' she exclaimed. 'And a room full of press men ain't going to bring me down'. Janis had just left the stage after a triumphant British debut which left most of the audience on their feet yelling for more. She hadn't expected it. Perhaps she believed too much about the traditional British reserve. 'We've been incredibly thrilled – this audience was great, American audiences are getting too jaded' she said, bouncing around the green room hardly able to contain her obvious delight.

Sadly, Joplin never returned. She died from a drug overdose a year after the show.

35. FRANK ZAPPA BANNED

In the lead-up to the release of Frank Zappa's surrealist movie *200 Motels*, an explicit portrayal of his life and sexual fantasies, the American star was due to conduct the soundtrack at the Hall in February 1971. But the concert, featuring the Royal Philharmonic Orchestra, was cancelled at the last minute, leaving 4,500 fans stranded. The Hall's letting manager Marion Herrod and its manager Frank Mundy read the libretto and found it 'obscene'. Two musicians walked out during rehearsals over expletives and sexual content in the lyrics, with the trumpet player John Wilbraham explaining his decision to leave by saying, 'The whole thing has revolted me.' A statement from the Hall explained that the show was cancelled on the grounds that 'the work contained a lot of unpleasant words … parts of the script were filthy. It was distasteful in the extreme.'

Furious, Zappa called the decision 'ridiculous', blaming it on a recent facelift at the building. He added, 'We are all very upset. It was alright for us to appear at the Albert Hall when the place was black and dirty. Now they've had the place cleaned up, they don't want to know us.' Four years later, Zappa took the Hall's management to court, claiming £8,000 in damages for breach of contract. The judge, on hearing one of the more explicit songs, asked 'Do I have to listen to that?' before ruling in the Hall's favour. The work finally premiered at the Hall on 29 October 2013, almost twenty years after Zappa's death.

36. Rock and Pop Hiatus

As the 1970s dawned, the Royal Albert Hall Council was becoming increasingly concerned about damage and rowdiness at pop and rock concerts. In 1972, after a particularly tumultuous year, it was decided that the Hall would no longer accept bookings from pop and rock acts. According to the press release announcing the decision, only one out of twenty-three such shows 'passed without disorder' in 1971, with 'vandalism and unruly behaviour' blighting concerts by Deep Purple, Yes, Gordon Lightfoot, Mott the Hoople, the Byrds and others. On one occasion, the Council noted, 'some members of the audience in second tier boxes became so enthusiastic and jumped and stamped around so much that the ceilings in two boxes in the grand tier below fell in. It is for reasons like this that we here do not like concerts at which the audience stamps and dances.'

Staff, the Council pointed out, had refused to work at these events, having suffered verbal and even physical abuse from fans. 'Mass hysteria is deliberately incited and encouraged by the performers,' read the notes. 'This results in large numbers of the audience leaving their seats and attempting to reach the platform, sometimes breaking down doors in the process.'

Mott the Hoople had been banned even before the new ruling – when the group played the Hall in July 1971, £1,467 of damage was recorded (over £8,000 today).

Among the first casualties of the new guidelines was the rock opera *Tommy*, due to be performed by the Who on 9 December 1972 with guest stars Rod Stewart, Steve Winwood, Ringo Starr and Richard Harris. Deemed 'unsavoury', *Tommy* would wait seventeen years, until 1989, to make its debut. In 2015, to mark fifty years of the Who, the Royal Albert Hall presented frontman Roger Daltrey and Pete Townshend with a framed apology, which read: 'We would like to take this opportunity to apologise for banning your show here on 9 December 1972. We've had a long think and, on reflection, you're welcome back any time.' Daltrey, who found the apology 'extremely funny', has since received a Royal

Albert Hall Star, located under the canopy outside the building.

While the ruling stayed in place for three years, some bands slipped through the net, including ABBA, whose 1977 gig garnered three and half million postal applications. In 1982, a new chief executive relaxed the restrictions and, a year later, a charity concert featuring Steve Winwood, Jimmy Page, Jeff Beck, Eric Clapton and Bill Wyman was staged, signalling an end to the ban.

37. OL' BLUE EYES

Frank Sinatra first played the Hall in 1975, but on his return in the spring of 1977 he broke records by selling out an eight-night run, with profits from the opening night going to the National Society for the Prevention of Cruelty for Children. The opening night was attended by Princess Margaret and Sinatra's ex-wife Ava Gardner, and the American legend went through a playlist of his classics, including 'Night and Day', 'The Lady is A Tramp' and 'My Way'. In fact, he so enthralled his devoted fans that they started circulating a petition to change the venue's name 'The Francis Albert Hall'. Chris Marshall, who was at one of the 1977 gigs, recalled: 'Most vividly I remember part way through the concert a lady walking the length of the hall and presenting Francis Albert with a pillow on which she had embroidered 'Be Reasonable … Do It My Way '.

Sinatra maintained a lifelong love of the Hall, headlining thirty-three times in total. In April 1989, he was joined by fellow legends Liza Minnelli and Sammy Davies Jr for Frank, Liza and Sammy: The Ultimate Event, which ran for five nights and featured the trio singing their greatest hits, accompanied by a forty-piece orchestra conducted by Frank Sinatra Jr. Each artist performed a thirty-minute set, after which all three united for a magnificent thirty-minute medley including 'But the World Goes 'Round', 'Witchcraft' and 'I've Got You Under My Skin'. Such was the demand for tickets that all five concerts sold out before even being advertised, and police had to erect crush barriers outside the Hall to hold back the crowds.

The shows marked the start of the British leg of a tour that visited twenty-seven cities around the world. Sadly, Sammy Davis Jr was suffering from cancer at the time, and died the following year – these were his final UK performances. Sinatra returned to headline for six nights from 26 to 31 May 1992.

38. MUSIC FOR MONTSERRAT

The eruption of the Soufrière Hills Volcano on Montserrat on 25 June 1997 claimed nineteen lives and devastated many communities. Beatles producer

George Martin, who had a house and studio on the Caribbean island, was
determined to raise money for the its stricken population, and decided to
organise a benefit concert that would bring together some of the biggest names
in pop and rock.

On September 15, rock legends including Ray Cooper, Carl Perkins, Sting,
Elton John and Paul McCartney took to the stage at the Royal Albert Hall for
Music For Montserrat. Mark Knopfler combined forces with Eric Clapton
and Phil Collins to perform the Dire Straits classic 'Money For Nothing',
and all the artists joined McCartney for renditions of 'Hey Jude' and an
unrehearsed 'Kansas City'. With tickets priced between £25 and £60, the
telecommunications company BSkyB donating the pay-per-view fee, and
a bestselling DVD, the event raised £1.5 million. The money was used for
immediate relief as well as a new cultural centre, which was gifted to the
islanders on its completion in 2006.

39. CELEBRATING MUSIC OF BLACK ORIGIN

The Music of Black Origin (MOBO) Awards have been held at the Hall on six
occasions, from 1998 to 1999 and again from 2003 to 2006. The star-studded
events, with hosts including Gina Yashere, Bill Bellamy, Coolio, Mos Def, Blu
Cantrell, Akon and Lil' Kim, have provided many memorable moments over the
years. In 1998, a heavily pregnant Mel B hosted the show and also performed,
and a year later she was joined on the stage by fellow Spice Girl Victoria
Beckham as a guest presenter, while husband David watched from the audience.
Tina Turner was another performer in 1999, and she also picked up the Lifetime
Achievement Award. It was her first time back at the Hall since she supported the
Rolling Stones in 1966 and, in her acceptance speech, she said: 'Black music has
finally been recognised. I've been in the business since 1960 and to my knowledge
black music has never been rewarded in this way.'

In 2003, 50 Cent turned up two hours late to collect three awards – Best Hip-
Hop Act, Best Single for 'In Da Club' and Best Album for *Get Rich Or Die
Tryin'* – delaying his own Wembley gig in the process. He arrived on stage to
collect his awards with a posse of ten, all with their faces covered with bandanas.
Other memorable moments include Kanye West receiving a record seven
nominations in 2004, and the tenth-anniversary celebration in 2005, at which
Lauryn Hill, Ms. Dynamite, Public Enemy and Kano all performed – Kano
would go on to headline the Hall in 2019. Rita Marley collected a posthumous
Icon Award for her late husband Bob at the tenth-anniversary event, while his

'Thanks to Roger and Teenage Cancer Trust, I've had some of the best nights I've ever had on a UK stage. The people who run the charity are amazing and the kids are an inspiration.' NOEL GALLAGHER

youngest son Damian won Best Reggae Act on the same night. In 2006, Rihanna performed at the ceremony, where she won the Best R&B Act, while Beyoncé was booed for staying away despite winning three gongs.

40. A TOUCHING TRIBUTE

On 29 November 2002 – the first anniversary of George Harrison's death – his closest friends and collaborators came together to honour him with a charity gig. Organised by widow Olivia and son Dhani, and under the musical direction of long-term friend Eric Clapton, A Concert for George featured a supergroup led by Clapton and ELO's Jeff Lynne, with celebrity guests Tom Petty, Joe Brown and former Beatles bandmates Paul McCartney and Ringo Starr, the latter two performing together for the first time since the break-up of the Fab Four. Among the many tracks written by Harrison performed at the gig were 'While My Guitar Gently Weeps', 'Something' and 'My Sweet Lord'.

Comic relief was provided by Monty Python members Terry Gilliam, Eric Idle, Michael Palin and Terry Jones, who performed a rendition of 'The Lumberjack Song' that featured a 'guest Mountie', Tom Hanks. Ravi Shankar introduced Harrison to the sitar, which was to become so influential in Harrison's later music. At A Concert for George, Shankar introduced a new composition written specifically for the occasion, performing it with his daughter Anoushka.

The event was a fitting tribute to the former Beatle, who laid the foundation for charity gigs such as Live Aid when he and Shankar staged the Concert for Bangladesh at New York's Madison Square in August 1971, attracting an audience of 40,000.

41. CHANGING LIVES

The annual Teenage Cancer Trust gigs, which raise money to provide treatment for young sufferers in the UK, are among the fifty charity performances that take place each year at the Hall. Conceived by Roger Daltrey in 2000, the first gig featured The Who, Paul Weller and Noel Gallagher. That initial show quickly grew into a week of events, and over the years the shows have featured legends such as Coldplay, Tom Jones, Kasabian, Arctic Monkeys, Paul McCartney, Pulp and Take That, as well as comedy stars including Kevin Bridges, Jo Brand and Romesh Ranganathan.

Ed Sheeran made his Royal Albert Hall debut in aid of the Teenage Cancer Trust in March 2014 to a thunderous reception, tweeting afterwards, 'Royal Albert Hall! It's good to be back gigging in the UK.' He returned three years later, supported by Busted, to perform a second gig for the charity. Since the concerts began, over £30 million has been raised for the Trust, which gives care and support to young people between thirteen and twenty-four years old from the moment they are diagnosed with cancer. The money has helped the Trust build, develop and maintain twenty-eight specialist cancer units in NHS hospitals across the UK, with over sixty nursing and support staff. Daltrey, who is the Trust's honorary patron, has spoken of his pleasure in what the gigs have accomplished:

> I am incredibly proud of what we have already achieved and am inspired about what we will accomplish together. Over the years I've been lucky enough to be part of many very memorable moments in the show's history, such as playing a surprise support set for Richard Ashcroft with Paul Weller, Kelly Jones and Liam and Noel Gallagher, seeing Little Britain's first live performance, and the Kaiser Chiefs opening up for Franz Ferdinand before taking the music world by storm. Within these memories of unique collaborations and musical firsts are the faces of the incredible young people I have met. Over the years I have met many young people with cancer and, like Teenage Cancer Trust, I believe that they shouldn't have to stop being teenagers just because they have this disease. They have helped me understand that they are young people first, cancer patients second, and I am always struck by their enthusiasm, positivity and their lust for life.

42. KING OF BLUES

B.B. King was 85 years old when he played the Albert Hall in 2011, forty-two years after he had first graced its stage. The US blues legend was joined by Ronnie Wood, Derek Trucks, Susan Tedeschi and Slash, with Mick Hucknall as guest vocalist. His first appearance, in April 1969, had seen him co-headlining with Fleetwood Mac, with Max Jones of *Melody Maker* writing a rave review:

> B.B. King spelled out the blues for a large, rapturous crowd at London's Royal Albert Hall last week. It was at Tuesday's opening of a well-varied package show which began with Sonny Terry and Brownie McGhee, followed by Duster Bennett. The second half was shared by Fleetwood Mac and King, and after B.B.'s high-voltage performance nobody seemed to want to go home. He appeared to be as affected by the welcome as we were by his subtly controlled

OVERLEAF: Florence + the Machine performing at the Teenage Cancer Trust concert, 24 March 2009.

vocal and instrumental art. From the beginning of his 'Every Day I Have
The Blues' to his final encore, B.B. and his fine tight band projected swing,
electrifying feeling, a highly professional polish and a kind of charm which is
not all that common among blues artists.

In total, King appeared at the Hall eleven times. He passed away in 2015, so
the 2011 gig turned out to be his last, but a number of photos around the Hall
remain as a tribute to him, and he also appears in Peter Blake's mural, *Appearing
at the Royal Albert Hall*. Many other blues artists have played the Hall, including

Bo Diddley, Jools Holland, Joe Bonamassa, John Mayall, Robert Cray, Rory Gallagher and Bobby Bland. The Hall also hosted Lead Belly Fest in 2015, and BluesFest in 2013 and 2014.

43. STARMAN

David Bowie's only verified appearance at the Hall was not as a headliner. The rock legend was a surprise guest at David Gilmour's show on 29 May 2006, duetting with the Pink Floyd singer on 'Arnold Layne' and 'Comfortably Numb'. It was the last ever UK appearance for the Ziggy Stardust singer, who died in January 2016 at the age of sixty-nine, but he was remembered on 29 July that year with a Prom in his honour. A review of the occasion in *The Times* read:

> As befits a man whose songs spanned so many eras, styles and genres, Bowie's own output was given a pretty eclectic make-over. At times the multi-talented ensemble underpinning the whole show – André de Ridder's Berlin-based Stargaze collective – verged into industrial noise or Stockhausen-style avant-garde clusters. The height of esoteric whimsy, as well as male falsetto, was reached when the French countertenor Philippe Jaroussky turned 'Always Crashing in the Same Car' into some sort of latter-day Debussy chanson. Other classics were thunderously reimagined. Along with Marc Almond, 5,000 voices attempted the perilous octave leap in 'Starman'. The Albert Hall organ added a spine-shuddering blast of Victorian gothic to the stunning Anna Calvi rendition of 'Lady Grinning Soul'.

It is thought that Bowie may have performed at A Gala Night Variety Concert, in aid of the National Society for Mentally Handicapped Children and St. Patrick's Island Building Fund, on 12 March 1970, although the show was not recorded. As a guest, he attended the 1985 Fashion Aid benefit concert at the Hall, and also Diana Ross's headline show in 1973. In addition, he made an exclusive Fashion Rocks video remix for the finale of the 2003 Fashion Rocks fundraiser.

44. IT'S A RAP

After a two-year 'retirement', Jay-Z headlined the Royal Albert Hall's first ever hip-hop show on 27 September 2006, as part of his Water for Life tour. The rapper's arrival was heralded by a black curtain draped across the stage, which dropped to reveal the Hustler Symphony Orchestra. They played Jay-Z in with an intro that culminated in Russell Crowe's famous Gladiator quote 'Are you not entertained?' thundering around the auditorium. The US star was joined by wife Beyoncé for the hits 'Crazy in Love' and 'Déjà Vu', but the big surprise of the evening was the guest spot by Gwyneth Paltrow, who was celebrating her twenty-fourth birthday, and duetted with Jay-Z on 'Song Cry' before the audience serenaded her with a chorus of 'Happy Birthday'. Chris Martin, Kano, Nas, Akala, Lupe Fiasco and Rick Ross also performed on the night. Since then the Hall has hosted many more hip-hop, grime and rap stars, including Wretch 32, Stormzy and Krept & Konan, who all took part in the Grime Prom on 12 August 2015.

45. BESTSELLER

While Adele has only headlined the Hall once, on 22 September 2011, this concert has been seen and heard by millions around the world. The DVD, *Adele: Live at the Royal Albert Hall*, has sold more than three million copies worldwide, and holds the record for the most weeks spent at number one in the United States for a music DVD by a female artist. Featuring tracks from Adele's hit albums, 19 and 21, as well as a cover of Bonnie Raitt's 'I Can't Make You Love Me', the ninety minutes of footage also include behind-the-scenes segments. The film was screened in twenty-six cinemas across the UK before going on sale, and Adele's live version of 'Set Fire to the Rain' from the event won the Grammy Award for Best Pop Solo Performance at the 55th Annual Grammy Awards.

Other notable headliners include Kylie Minogue, who performed her A Kylie Christmas concerts in 2015 and 2016; Joan Armatrading, who has played the Hall five times; and Muse, who headlined in 2018. Paul Weller is another fan of the Hall, headlining twenty-three times between 1993 and 2017.

COMEDY AT THE HALL

46. POST-WAR HOPE

Comedy has been hosted at the Hall since the 1940s, with the first one-man stand-alone show, Bob Hope Independence Day Concert, being staged on 4 July 1945, just a month after the end of the Second World War in Europe. With war still raging in the Pacific, US troops stationed in the UK were still awaiting orders to return home. Bob Hope, who entertained soldiers on fifty tours with the United Service Organizations between 1941 and 1991, led the concert, which was attended by 10,000 military personnel, and joked, 'We get a big kick out of coming to these out-of-the-way places.' Hope's last appearance at the Hall was in 1994 for a retrospective of his life, told through clips and stories. At the age of ninety-one, frail and deaf, he still made audiences roar with laughter, at one point almost falling in the orchestra pit.

47. NOW FOR SOMETHING COMPLETELY DIFFERENT

In 1977, April Fool's Day brought the aptly named Nobody's Fools: Rock with Laughter gig, in aid of the National Association for Mental Health, better known as Mind. Presented by Bob Harris, Sally James and Mike Smith, the 'rock' was provided by Alexis Korner, Animals keyboardist Alan Price, Bonzo Dog Band founder Vivian Stanshall and Liverpool group the Scaffold, while the 'laughter' came courtesy of Jasper Carrott, Neil Innes and the comedy superstars Monty Python. Two years after their hit movie *Monty Python and the Holy Grail*, John Cleese, Michael Palin, Terry Jones and Graham Chapman brought the house down, and not for the last time. On 23 October 2009, to mark the fortieth anniversary of the first *Monty Python's Flying Circus*, Eric Idle, Michael Palin, Terry Jones and Terry Gilliam starred in the UK premiere of *Not the Messiah (He's a Very Naughty Boy)*, Idle's oratorio based on Monty Python's *Life of Brian*.

Comedy and charity have long gone hand in hand at the Hall, with the Teenage Cancer Trust gigs showcasing talent including Jimmy Carr, Russell Brand, Romesh Ranganathan and Miranda Hart over the last twenty years. These gigs have also seen appearances from Sara Pascoe, Russell Howard, Jo Brand, Alan Carr, Noel Fielding, Frankie Boyle, Micky Flanagan, Tim Minchin and Kevin Bridges, to name a few. In 2015, Bridges joked that the Hall was the poshest venue he had ever played, adding, 'I never thought I'd be welcoming people to the Albert Hall unless I had a high-visibility jacket on.'

In 2006 and 2008, the Secret Policeman's Ball, held in aid of Amnesty International, saw the likes of James Corden, Eddie Izzard, Jo Brand, Shappi Khorsandi, Sean Lock, the Mighty Boosh and Omid Djalili raising the laughs. They were joined by American stars including Sarah Silverman and Chevy Chase, as well as actors Meera Syal, Richard E. Grant, Shobna Gulati and Jeremy Irons. The 2008 Secret Policeman's Ball marked the start of Amnesty International's celebrations of the sixtieth anniversary of the Universal Declaration of Human Rights.

OVERLEAF: Programme for 'Nobody's Fools - Rock with Laughter' in aid of The British Institute for the Achievement of Human Potential & Mind, 1 April 1977 and the handbill for Late Night Laughs, September–December 2015.

NOBODY'S FOOLS

OR

ROCK WITH LAUGHTER

CONCERT

Presented by Larry Westland

IN AID OF THE BRITISH INSTITUTE FOR THE ACHIEVEMENT OF HUMAN POTENTIAL
AND MIND (NATIONAL ASSOCIATION FOR MENTAL HEALTH)

SPONSORED BY EMI TAPES LTD

SUPPORTED BY RADIO LUXEMBOURG

PROGRAMME·50p

Dick

CARL DONNELLY & PHIL WANG

MARCEL LUCONT & DAN CLARK

RICHARD HERRING

ED GAMBLE

BEC HILL & MATT FORDE

LATE NIGHT LAUGHS
ROYAL ALBERT HALL
ELGAR ROOM

FELICITY WARD & JOHN ROBINS

MIKE WOZNIAK

ROBERT AUTON & IAIN STIRLING

MARK SMITH • **HOLLY WALSH**

LIAM WILLIAMS & MARK COOPER

NISH KUMAR & ERIC LAMPAERT

PHIL ELLIS

AISLING BEA

ADAM HESS

LLOYD GRIFFITH

SEAN MCLOUGHLIN

DAVID TRENT

ALUN COCHRANE

ANDY ZALTZMAN

JULIAN DEANE

48. FUNNY GIRL

With two sell-out runs of fifteen shows, in both 1993 and 1996, Victoria Wood holds the record for the longest run of shows by a comedian. She returned to the Hall for another run in 2001, when she signed the visitor book with 'This will be the nearest I ever get to working with [pianist and conductor] Vladimir Ashkenazy. Back for the third (and last?) time.' In fact, she did return twice more – on 14 April 2002 for a one-off charity performance to raise money for the King's Head Theatre in Islington, and on 17 November 2009 to host a fundraising night in celebration of thirty-five years of the theatre charity Chickenshed. In total, she played the venue forty-seven times.

49. CRACKING COMICS

In 2017, three years after his Hall debut with his Wonderbox tour, critically acclaimed comedy star Russell Howard returned with the Round the World tour. The ten-night sell-out stint, from 1 March to 10 March, broke the record for the longest consecutive run by a performer, a mark previously shared by Frank Sinatra and Barry Manilow. In an interview a year later, Howard said, 'I was really proud. The headline in the *Evening Standard* was "Ol' Blue Eyes beaten by

OPPOSITE: Victoria Wood outside the Royal Albert Hall, 21 September 1993.

RIGHT: Russell Howard on the first of four nights at the Royal Albert Hall on his Wonderbox tour, 14 April 2014.

Young Lazy Eyes" so all the glamour was instantly robbed from me.'

In another first, Russell played his 2017 gigs in the round, performing on a circular stage in the centre of the arena. 'It's such a beautiful shape and I wanted to do something different,' he explained. 'I thought it would be quite cool to make it more intimate. It was really great, and I had to figure out how to play to each side. It made it unique and interesting. It was a different way of doing it – rather than having 5,000 people in front of you, you have them closer to you.'

Naming the Royal Albert Hall as the 'best venue in the world', he said: 'When people walk in you're hit with this magnificence and it creates its own atmosphere. They're already excited then they walk into this palace and you can feel them going "Oh my God". Everyone is taking selfies because the venue is so beautiful.'

Other star comics to play the venue have included Victor Borge, Billy Connolly and Bill Bailey. In the last decade, the Hall has also seen headline performances from Joan Rivers, Al Murray, Dave Chappelle and Jon Stewart, Bill Burr and, in 2018, a live podcast of *My Dad Wrote a Porno.*

50. OFF THE MAIN STAGE

Not all the laughs are in the auditorium. Over the last decade, the Elgar Room has played host to more intimate comedy shows, such as Late Night Laughs, which kicked off in 2015. Its first year saw eleven shows hosted by Richard Herring, Ed Gamble and Ray Peacock, and featuring incredible talents such as Holly Walsh, Sofie Hagen, Phil Wang, Andy Zaltzman and Aisling Bea. The series has regularly included shows by Arabs Are Not Funny, a collective of Muslim stand-ups including Zahra Barri, Mohamed Omar, Fatiha El-Ghorri, Marouen Mraihi and Sarah Agha.

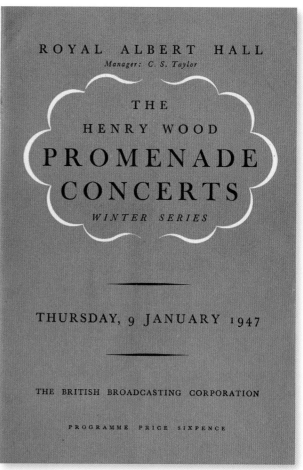

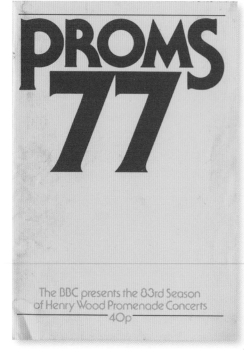

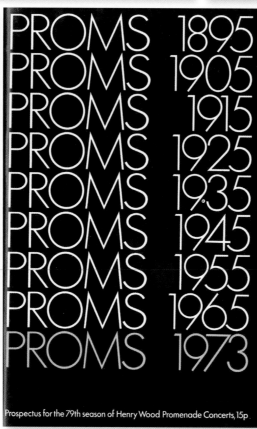

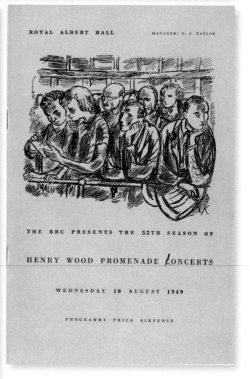

6 CLASSICAL

Although the Royal Albert Hall is known as the home of the BBC Proms, there are many, many more classical-music events taking place under the famous dome, from the annual performance of the *Messiah* by George Frederic Handel to the premieres of works by such famous composers as Giuseppe Verdi and Antonín Dvořák.

51. FINDING A VOICE

The opening of the Royal Albert Hall provided London with the perfect venue for grand choral concerts. When French composer Charles-François Gounod conducted just such a concert in June 1871, the Royal Commission was so impressed that it invited him to form a resident choir, with himself as conductor. Auditions were held, over 1,000 members were signed up, and the Royal Albert Hall Choral Society staged its first concert on 8 May 1872, watched by Queen Victoria.

The following year, the celebrated choirmaster Joseph Barnby took over, merging his existing choir with the Society. In its review of the musical highlights of 1888, *Hazell's Annual Cyclopedia* recorded that 'The Royal Albert Hall Choral Society, in May, gave a performance of [Arthur Sullivan's] *The Golden Legend* by command of the Queen, who was present, and Mr Barnby's force is henceforward to be called the Royal Choral Society.' Barnby continued to lead the choir until his death in 1896, staging hugely popular productions of Handel's *Messiah*, inviting Verdi to conduct the British premiere of his *Requiem* in 1875, and engaging Dvořák to conduct his *Stabat Mater* nine years later.

By January 1899, the *Musical Times* counted 242 sopranos, 174 contraltos, 174 tenors, 236 basses and 16 so-called 'superintendents' in the Society – a total of 842 singing members – who were 'arranged as two separate choirs, one on each

ABOVE: A drawing of
the audience at the Royal
Albert Hall Choral
Society's first concert,
8 May 1872.

OPPOSITE: Ticket for
the Royal Choral Society
(Twenty-Ninth Season
1899-1900) Handel's
'Messiah' New Years Day,
1 January 1900.

side of the organ. At concerts the ladies wore white dresses, those of the right choir adding red sashes and those of the left choir blue ones.'

Among the successes for the Society were its hugely popular annual performances of Samuel Coleridge-Taylor's *The Song of Hiawatha*, which ran from 1924 to 1953. In 1928, Malcolm Sargent, acclaimed as the finest British choral conductor of his generation, took over as conductor, steering the Society through the Hall's closure during the Second World War, when it decamped to the nearby Queen's Hall for morale-boosting performances of the *Messiah*, along with Felix Mendelssohn's *Elijah* and Edward Elgar's *The Dream of Gerontius*.

The Society returned to the Royal Albert Hall after the destruction of the Queen's Hall in May 1941 during an air raid. After the war it began recruiting new members and touring overseas, with concerts in the United States, France, Poland, Switzerland and Portugal. There were premieres of works by Raymond Premru, Anthony Milner and Geoffrey Burgon, and contributions to the 'Classic Rock' and 'Hooked On Classics' series of recordings, the first with pop songs given classical arrangements, the other with discofied classical pieces.

Under current musical director Richard Cooke, the Society has gone from strength to strength, co-operating with charities for its gala concerts, and packing the house out for the annual carol concerts, which have now run for over a hundred years. It also seeks to bring little-known music to wider attention, including the rarely performed *Damnation of Faust* and *Grande Messe des Morts both* by Hector Berlioz, as well as Gustav Mahler's symphonies and Franz Schubert's masses, which have been performed to critical acclaim.

52. COMING OF THE *MESSIAH*

Handel's *Messiah* was first performed at the Hall on the 22 June 1871, and has returned every year since, with the exception of 1940 and 1941, when the Hall was closed due to concerns about air raids. The debut performance by the National Choral Society and Band included an amazing 1,000 performers, and was one of five *Messiah* concerts during the Hall's opening year, including a Christmas recital. From 1873, the annual shows were performed by the Royal Choral Society under Joseph Barnby. Although the oratorio was always associated with Christmas, Barnby also recognised the *Messiah*'s relevance to Easter, and in 1876 he began the tradition of a Good Friday performance, which continues to this day. As of December 2019, the *Messiah* has been performed in full in the Hall over five hundred times, to a total of five million concert-goers.

53. ARMCHAIR LISTENING

Among the biggest classical events of the Hall's early years was the Wagner Festival, which comprised nine concerts during May 1877. Richard Wagner was originally planning to conduct a two-hundred-strong orchestra in performances of his own works in the first half, before handing over to the celebrated Hungarian conductor Hans Richter for his UK debut in the second half. But in rehearsals Wagner, overwhelmed by the scale of the Hall, made three false starts on his opera *The Flying Dutchman* before throwing down the baton in despair and demanding Richter take over. It was decided that Wagner would only conduct the first piece in each concert and, for the rest of the evening, the audience was treated to the sight of the German composer hunched in an armchair on the stage.

54. HOPE AND GLORY

Sir Edward Elgar conducted at the Hall on eighteen occasions, making him the third most performed composer at the Hall after Tchaikovsky and then Handel. Perhaps his most famous appearance as a conductor at the hall was as one of seven conductors at the famous Titanic Band Memorial Concert in 1912. In July 1914, the great British composer conducted his own 'Pomp and Circumstance March No. 1' – better known as 'Land of Hope and Glory' – in front of a packed audience, who waved specially made Union Jacks in front of George V and Queen Mary – the famous composition is now an integral part of the Last Night of The Proms. Elgar also conducted at a special concert to celebrate the Hall's fiftieth Birthday in 1921, and in 1932, at the age of seventy-five, he conducted a sixteen-year-old Yehudi Menuhin in his *Violin Concerto in B Minor* at a Sunday afternoon concert that also featured conductor Sir Thomas Beecham.

HANDEL'S "MESSIAH." 3
H 244 STALL.
EVENING DRESS.
1st JAN., 1900. TO BE RETAINED.

Stage capacity

For a choral concert, a maximum of 426 performers is allowed on stage Risers – platforms placed on stage for performances – are used for big choirs.

A total of 303 choristers can be seated on the risers in a three-aisle configuration, with 123 performers on the flat of the stage.

If more performers are required, the capacities of the stalls to the left and the right of the stage are reduced by the number of extra performers.

BELOW: Handel's Messiah
at the Royal Albert Hall,
Friday 21 December
2018.

OPPOSITE: Programme
cover for the Wagner
Festival, 7-29 May 1877.

Classical

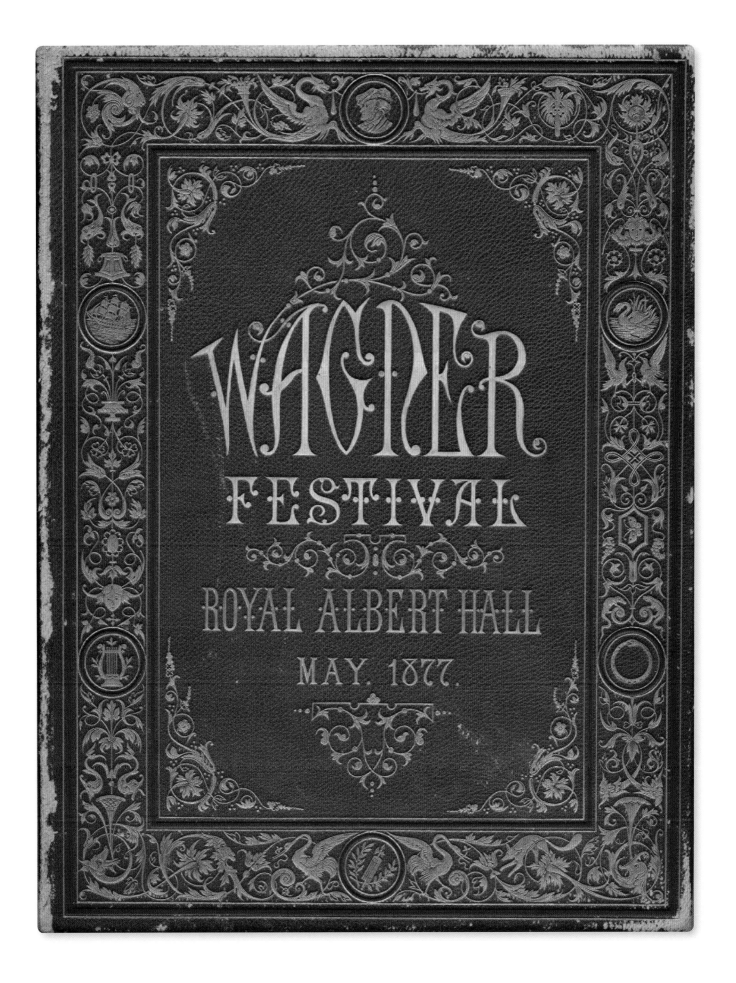

WAGNER
FESTIVAL
ROYAL ALBERT HALL
MAY. 1877.

Elgar was one of the first composers to record his own work, from 1925, after the invention of the electric microphone led to huge leaps in sound quality, he made a series of gramophone records, choosing the Royal Albert Hall Orchestra to perform his *Enigma Variations*. A performance studio in the Hall is named the Elgar Room in his honour.

55. The Band Played On

As the RMS *Titanic* sank in the icy Atlantic Ocean in the early hours of 15 April 1912, claiming over 1,500 lives, bandmaster Wallace Henry Hartley and seven other musicians stayed at their posts and continued to play. These heroic men, who all perished in the disaster, were honoured at the Titanic Band Memorial Concert just over a month later, on Empire Day, Friday 24 May.

Elgar was among seven legendary conductors, including Henry Wood and Thomas Beecham, who lead 'the greatest professional orchestra ever assembled'. The 473-strong orchestra comprised members of seven London orchestras including the Philharmonic Orchestra and the Royal Opera Orchestra. Members of the London Symphony Orchestra had a particularly poignant reason to take part in the Memorial Concert – they had been booked on the *Titanic* ahead of a three-week tour of the United States and Canada, but rescheduling meant they left a week earlier.

Empire Day was a public holiday, so the auditorium was full for the afternoon event, with an audience of 7,750 composed of dignitaries, members of the public and families of the bereaved, in seats costing from one shilling in the gallery (around £3 today) to three guineas for a seat in a box (around £190 today). Ada Crossley sang Mendelssohn's 'O Rest in the Lord' from *Elijah*, and the rest of the programme consisted of solemn orchestral items including works by Elgar, Tchaikovsky and Wagner, as well as Frédéric Chopin's *Funeral March* and Arthur Sullivan's *In Memoriam*. For the finale, the whole audience rose to their feet to sing 'Nearer, My God, to Thee', the hymn Hartley and his band were reportedly playing as the ship went down. Most of the audience and many of the orchestra were moved to tears.

Several survivors recalled hearing this famous hymn as the *Titanic* listed, and the opening notes are carved on the Titanic Musicians' Memorial in Southampton and on Hartley's Lancashire grave, but many have disputed whether this was the last tune that the Titanic band actually played. Archibald Gracie, one of the last survivors to leave the ship, did not hear it, and the wireless operator Harold Bride – another survivor who was washed off as the ship went

Opposite: Handbill
for Royal Albert Hall
Sunday Concerts (1933-
1934 Season) - Yehudi
Menuhin, 10 December
1933.

under – remembered hearing 'Autumn', a popular waltz tune of the era. What
has never been disputed is that the brave band played on, even as the ocean took
them to their watery graves.

To mark the one-hundredth anniversary of the sinking in 2012, the Royal
Albert Hall hosted the premiere of *Titanic 3D*, attended by the film's director
James Cameron and by its lead actress Kate Winslet.

56. Boy Wonder

On 10 November 1929, a 'small flaxen haired boy, wearing an open shirt, with
short sleeves, shorts and black socks and shoes' took to the stage at the Albert
Hall with his violin and, according to a contemporary newspaper report, 'held
thousands of people spellbound'. He was American prodigy Yehudi Menuhin,
and he was just twelve years old at the time.

For over two hours, Menuhin delighted the audience with a programme
'capable of taxing the greatest artist, yet he remained as cool and assured as a
man', the report continued. 'Seldom have such scenes of enthusiasm been seen
at the Albert Hall at the end of a concert. People flocked up to the platform, and
firemen had to keep the crowd back. The cheers and applause were deafening.
Men threw their hats in the air and women waved their hands and handkerchiefs.
The audience refused to leave even after Menuhin had given three encores, the
lights had been turned out, the piano closed, and the young artist had come back
in his coat to bow his thanks.'

Eventually, the young musician came back onto the stage for one more encore
before the lights were switched off again and the audience finally filed out.
He still holds the Hall record for the number of encores. Menuhin would go
on to play at the Hall 115 times over eight decades, including four wartime
fundraising concerts that, combined with other concerts across the UK during
the conflict , raised £30,000 for charities. After the war, right up until the
1980s, the violinist headlined annually, sharing the stage with the conductor
Adrian Boult, the London Philharmonic Orchestra, violinist David Oistrakh
and instrumentalist Ravi Shankar, among many others. His sister, Hephzibah
Menuhin, was a talented pianist and performed with him at the Hall on thirteen
occasions, including at a concert to mark the Festival of Britain on 9 May 1951,
and at three Proms. After her death in January 1981, Menuhin performed with
the Royal Philharmonic Orchestra at a tribute concert to his sister.

Menuhin's final appearance at the Hall was in December 1998, when he
conducted the Philharmonic Orchestra playing Ludwig van Beethoven's

ROYAL ALBERT HALL

Manager - CHARLES B. COCHRAN

Sunday, DECEMBER 10 at 3

HAROLD HOLT PRESENTS

YEHUDI

MENUHIN

ONLY APPEARANCE THIS SEASON

PROGRAMME

Sonata No 7 in C minor, Opus, 30, No. 2	BEETHOVEN
Sonata No. 3 in C major ...	BACH
(Violin alone)	
Concerto in D major	PAGANINI
Hungarian Dances	BRAHMS-JOACHIM
Spanish Dances	SARASATE
Introduction and Rondo Capriccioso, Opus 28	SAINT-SAENS

At the Piano - - WALTER BOHLE

STEINWAY PIANO   "HIS MASTER'S VOICE" RECORDS

TICKETS (including Tax) : Reserved : Stalls 21/-, 15/-, 12/- 8/6.   Arena 12/-, 9/-, 6/-
Lower Orchestra 7/6. Balcony 6-. Upper Orchestra 6/-.   Unres.: Gallery 3/6.
From Box Office, Royal Albert Hall, Chappell's Box Offices, 50 New Bond Street and Queen's Hall and Usual Agents
A stamped addressed envelope must accompany all applications for Tickets by post.   P.T.O.

BELOW: Grand Pageant
of The Empire and Her
Allies - New Year Festival,
1 January 1943.

OPPOSITE: Tenor Juan
Diego Flórez performs
Rule, Britannia! with the
BBC Singers, the BBC
Symphony Chorus and the
BBC Symphony Orchestra
conducted by Sakari
Oramo at the Last Night
of the Proms 2016.

The Hall in the War

When the Second World War broke out on 1 September 1939, the Hall was immediately closed, for fear of air attacks. But eighteen months later, in May 1941, it reopened following an appeal from the Hall's Council to the police. It was then used for patriotic rallies and morale-boosting concerts, as well as for secret government meetings.

The reopening was subject to several strict conditions:

The Hall was only used during daylight hours

Only 5,000 people could attend an event

The balcony and gallery could be not used

Audiences could shelter in the corridors if an air-raid warning was sounded

Some windows had to have anti-splintering treatment or wooden shutters fitted

The glass dome was blacked out with paint

Air-raid warnings were printed on every programme advising concert-goers of local air-raid shelter points, including the basement corridors and the nearby pedestrian tunnel under Exhibition Road. A red light above the orchestra lit up if an air raid was signalled but, despite evacuation being encouraged, most preferred to take their chances and enjoy the music.

Symphony No. 9. He died four months later at the age of eighty-two. In November 1999, he was honoured with a memorial concert attended by Charles, the Prince of Wales, with the Yehudi Menuhin School Orchestra and Menuhin's son Jeremy, an accomplished pianist, playing.

57. ARRIVAL OF THE PROMS

The Proms was almost fifty years into its run when a German bomb forced a move from its original home at the Queen's Hall in nearby Fitzrovia. At eleven o'clock in the evening, on 10 May 1941, just hours after a matinee performance of Elgar's *Dream of Gerontius* conducted by Malcolm Sargent, the building was hit during a Luftwaffe air raid.

The Palace of Westminster, Westminster Abbey and the British Museum also suffered direct hits that night. The Auxiliary Fire Service struggled to cope with so many fires around London, and ran out of water. The roof of the Queen's Hall soon collapsed and its organ was completely destroyed. Henry Wood, who had conducted the Proms since the very first concert in 1895, was photographed in his three-piece suit and bow tie, hat in hand, astride the wreckage. In the rubble

of the building, the bronze bust of the conductor survived unscathed, and it is still placed in front of the Albert Hall's organ throughout the Proms today and decorated with a laurel crown on the Last Night.

Defiant in the face of adversity, Wood immediately declared: 'We must build another Queen's Hall.' This eventually proved impossible, and it was decided that the Proms would move to the Royal Albert Hall, which had twice the capacity of the original venue. The Albert Hall itself was saved from the worst of the Blitz, although it did suffer some collateral damage in October 1940, when the blasts from three separate bombs shattered the external windows.

58. MUSIC FOR THE MASSES

The new Proms season opened on 12 July 1941 and lasted for six weeks – the Hall has been their home ever since. *The Times* hailed the first night as a triumph, stating, 'The forty-seventh season of Promenade concerts conducted by Sir Henry Wood and the first to be given in the Albert Hall was begun on Saturday with every symptom of popular success.' After the season had closed, Wood wrote to one of Hall's executives, a Mr Askew, to rebook for the following year:

Classical

'During the hour before the concerts we used to muck around. We used to play cricket in the gallery with rolled-up balls of paper! We made paper aeroplanes out of the advertisements in the programme. We'd throw it from the gallery and hope it would reach the floor. We'd all cheer if it got further than the balcony!' .

ALISON JOHNSTON, A DEVOTED PROM-GOER SINCE THE 1960S

'I am very happy to have had this, my forty-seventh Prom, at the Royal Albert Hall and take the opportunity to thank you for all you have done, via your staff. I could not have believed I could settle down so happily away from my old home at the Queen's Hall.'

The Promenade Concerts, to give them their full title, were conceived by the impresario Robert Newman as a way of bringing classical music to the masses at affordable prices, with tickets starting at just a shilling. 'I am going to run nightly concerts and train the public by easy stages … Popular at first, gradually raising the standard until I have created a public for classical and modern music,' declared Newman. His dream of bringing classical music to all is still at the heart of the Proms. Around 1,300 standing tickets are issued, most of which go on sale on the day of the concert at a bargain rate. Every year thousands of 'Promenaders' flock to the Hall and, in recent years, they have also been able to attend Proms in the Park events around the country.

The BBC have broadcasted the Proms since 1927, apart from a brief spell at the start of the Second World War. Today every concert is broadcast live on the radio, as well as being live-streamed by the BBC.

59. LAST NIGHT OF THE PROMS

The Last Night of the Proms is the most popular concert of the season and comes with its own long-held traditions. The second half of the programme is a fixed sequence of set pieces, including 'Pomp and Circumstance March No. 1' (otherwise known as 'Land of Hope and Glory'), Henry Wood's *Fantasia on British Sea Songs*, 'Rule, Britannia!' and 'Jerusalem'. Many Prommers have their own moves to accompany the music, and the songs of *Fantasia* in particular elicit a variety of actions: bobbing up and down to the 'Hornpipe', the dabbing of eyes with hankies in the moving 'Tom Bowling', whistling along to 'See, the Conqu'ring Hero Comes' and swaying and humming to 'Home Sweet Home'. Famously, the rendition of 'Auld Lang Syne' at the end of the evening is accompanied by the entire audience linking arms. In a fine piece of pantomime, Wood would arrive for the concert's final pieces in a coat and scarf, carrying a hat, apparently impatient to leave, and urge the orchestra to rush

OPPOSITE: A historic performer in Regency costume serving food to Prommers at the Royal Albert Hall, 29 August 1959.

RIGHT: Jacob Banks and Wretch 32 performing with the BBC Concert Orchestra during Prom 37 of the BBC Proms at the Royal Albert Hall, 10 August 2013.

Classical

with breakneck speed through the 'Hornpipe' section of his *Fantasia*.

Wood began another beloved tradition when he made the first conductor's speech as the 1941 season came to close. A shy man who rarely addressed the audience for fear it would betray his class and detract from the inclusive message of the Proms, he was so moved by the first season in the Royal Albert Hall that he got up to thank the sponsors and loyal Prommers, without whom the season would not have been able to go ahead. The conductor's speech became a firm favourite under Wood's successor, the flamboyant showman Malcolm Sargent, whose witty speeches between 1947 and 1967 were hugely popular. In 1992, the much-loved conductor Andrew Davis surprised audiences by singing his speech.

The second half of the Last Night of the Proms has only been changed once, in 2001, when it fell just four days after the September 11 terrorist attacks in the United States. On this occasion, the familiar favourites were replaced by the finale from Beethoven's *Symphony No. 9*.

60. Stepping Up

During one Last Night, on the hot summer evening of 7 August 1974, the baritone Thomas Allen was overcome with the heat and fainted in the middle of his performance of Carl Orff's *Carmina Burana*. Ironically, his understudy was a doctor and was required to treat the ailing singer, leaving a gap in the programme. But music student Patrick McCarthy, who was in the audience, saved the day when he walked onto the stage and told its conductor, André Previn, 'I know this piece. I'll do it.' Having sung the piece several times at music college, he had just offered his services backstage, been handed a spare jacket and a score and directed towards the stage. Previn was understandably nervous about the impromptu performance but McCarthy gave a rousing rendition and received rapturous applause. Back home in Brighton his mother, listening on the radio, was astounded to hear her own son among the soloists .

61. First Lady of the Proms

New Yorker Marin Alsop became the first woman conductor of the Last Night of The Proms in 2013, and took up the baton again in 2015. In the interval, the Prommers decked out her podium with pink balloons reading, 'It's a Girl.' 'I thought it was really funny,' she later said. 'I felt it was very much in the spirit of the Last Night.' One thing that sets the Royal Albert Hall apart, Marin says, is the proximity of the audience to the performers. 'I love being so close to them and I love their

'When the BBC Proms season starts, there is a measurable change in tempo. Your life changes subtly; a kind of light comes into your diary. The Royal Albert Hall is such an exciting place, it's a wonderful arena. And there's a great communal feeling, which is cemented by the Prommers. Then the lights go down and the glamour starts. The orchestra is on stage and the conductor comes on. And this unbelievable sound comes from the stage. There is no disc, no radio, that can match the business of being there and having the sound come from the stage straight to your ears.'

DAVID ATTENBOROUGH, A LONG-TIME PROMS ATTENDEE, QUOTED IN 2019

exuberance and their enthusiasm. There is rarely a moment in life where everybody is there for the right reasons, to have a good time. That was really thrilling.'

The first female conductor ever at the Hall, however, was Antonia Brico, who led the London Philharmonic in a concert in 1946 at the invitation of Adrian Bolt. The Dutch-born pioneer, who succeeded in a male-dominated profession, once said, 'You're either born a musician or you're born not a musician. It has nothing to do with gender.'

62. ROCK MEETS PROMS

Soft Machine were the first rock band to perform at a Prom when they collaborated with electronics wizard Tim Souster in 1970. The avant-garde group were a huge hit with their combination of progressive rock and jazz, but not everyone was a fan. Drummer Robert Wyatt recalled:

> It was brave of [Souster] to invite us despite the withering contempt of the posh music establishment. Before our bit, I went out the back for a quick fag and then the doorman didn't want to let me back in. 'I've got to play in there,' I said. 'You must be kidding, son,' he said. 'They only have proper music in there.' Not that night they didn't!

63. THEMED PROMS

In recent years, the Proms have become ever more varied and experimental, reaching out to different cultures and influences around the world. In 2011, conductor Charles Hazlewood challenged top instrument-makers to make a whole orchestra from scrap as part of the BBC project Scrapheap Orchestra. The results included a cello made of plywood and two washing-up bowls; a double bass

created from parts of a car; and a violin fashioned from a toilet's waste pipe, with a bow that had once been an arrow. The BBC Concert Orchestra used these improvised instruments to play Tchaikovsky's *1812 Overture*.

A 'cracking' time was had at the 2012 Wallace & Gromit Prom, at which a new composition by Wallace – the grandly named *My Concerto in Ee Lad* – was performed, with contributions from his far brighter pooch. Even the weary, dog-eared Gromit raised an appreciative eyebrow at conductor Nicholas Collon, and the kids and parents couldn't help but smile. The second half of the programme saw a screening of Nick Park's animated film *A Matter of Loaf and Death*, shown with a live orchestral soundtrack for the first time.

Following the success of 2013's Urban Classic Prom, BBC Radio 1Xtra presented a celebration of the thriving urban-music scene two years later. Stormzy blew in to perform 'Know Me From' and Krept & Konan got the Proms in party spirit with their hit 'Freak of the Week'. That same year, Emeli Sandé and Kanika Kapoor were special guests for a night of Bollywood and bhangra music at the Asian Network Prom, at which Palak Muchhal and Benny Dayal represented the new wave of Bollywood.

A celebration of David Bowie's songs and music in 2016 was held to mark his

OPPOSITE: Marin Alsop
during the finale of the
Last Night of the Proms
2013.

death at the age of sixty-nine. Amongst those performing interpretive renditions of his work were Neil Hannon of the Divine Comedy with 'Station to Station', and singer-guitarist Anna Calvi with 'Lady Grinning Soul'.

The Tardis parked next to the bust of Henry Wood in advance of the 2008 Doctor Who Prom. Monsters and aliens from the much-loved television series invaded the stage, including the dreaded Daleks. The concert featured dramatic music from the series along with such powerful works as Gustav Holst's *The Planets* and Mark-Anthony Turnage's *Three Asteroids*, resulting in a spine-chilling experience. The Prom was presented by actress Freema Agyeman, who was playing the Doctor's companion at the time. It was such a success that the Doctor Who Prom was repeated during the 2010 and 2013 seasons.

64. GREAT BRITTEN

The composer and conductor Benjamin Britten made his Hall debut on the piano at the Proms in 1943, with the UK premiere of his *Scottish Ballad for Two Pianos and Orchestra*. It was the first of numerous appearances over his illustrious career, including a memorable performance in 1945, also as a pianist. He delighted the audience by playing Francis Poulenc's *Concerto in D Minor for Two Pianos and Orchestra* – with Poulenc himself on the second piano.

The Hall also saw the first concert-hall performance of Britten's *War Requiem*, performed by the London Symphony Orchestra and the Bach Choir on 9 January 1963. It was conducted by Britten and featured his partner Peter Pears, both of whom had founded the Aldeburgh Proms in 1948 along with the writer Eric Crozier. The eighty-five-minute piece had previously been performed on 30 May 1962 for the consecration of the new Coventry Cathedral, built after the original fourteenth-century church was all but destroyed in a bombing raid during the Second World War. Throughout the work Britten, a pacifist, interspersed Latin texts from the traditional Requiem Mass with poems by Wilfred Owen written during the First World War. For the premiere at Coventry Cathedral, Britten chose soloists Galina Vishnevskaya (a Russian), Peter Pears (an Englishman) and Dietrich Fischer-Dieskau (a German) to demonstrate a spirit of unity, but Vishnevskaya was prevented from travelling by the Soviet authorities, so the Northern Irish soprano Heather Harper stepped in and performed the role. Happily, Vishnevskaya was later allowed to travel to the UK to make an award-winning recording of the *Requiem*, and to perform at the Hall's concert. Britten made his final appearance at the Hall on 8 September 1971 at that year's Proms.

Opposite: Daleks at the Doctor Who Prom with the BBC National Orchestra of Wales at the Royal Albert Hall, 13 July 2013.

65. A Sound Investment

In May 1945, a young Jewish immigrant named Victor Hochhauser borrowed £200 from his father to stage a concert at the Royal Albert Hall. The twenty-two-year-old, who had previously organised just one piano concert, at London's Whitehall Theatre in aid of Second World War refugees, had the idea of regular Sunday evening concerts and initially spent £30 on hiring the Hall and £60 on booking the London Symphony Orchestra. The resulting series of concerts sold out, and involved such big names as the violinist Ida Haendel and pianists Eileen Joyce, Louis Kentner and Benno Moiseiwitsch. Hochhauser went on to become the most prolific promoter at the Hall.

One early booking was Yehudi Menuhin, whom he secured by asking established promoter Harold Holt for help. 'I asked him how to contact Yehudi Menuhin, who was his biggest money-spinner,' he later recalled, adding that Holt, thinking him a novice, gave Hochhauser a discount. 'Instead of charging me 1,000 guineas, he only charged me £1,000. He gave me Menuhin's phone number in 1947, and my association with him lasted until he died in 1999.' In 1946, he secured the conductor Thomas Beecham for a season of concerts. 'It all seemed so easy,' Hochhauser reflected many years later.

This audacious move was the start of a sixty-year career that saw Hochhauser and wife Lilian bringing famous musicians and dancers from the Soviet Union and Eastern European countries to delight UK audiences. During the Cold War, Victor made frequent trips behind the Iron Curtain, persuading Soviet authorities to allow talent such as the ballet dancer Rudolf Nureyev and the pianist Sviatoslav Richter to travel to London, as well as the Bolshoi and Kirov ballets – many of the performers became personal friends. Hochhauser later recalled:

Despite the Cold War, and however cold it was, with all the hundreds of companies that we brought here and sent to Russia, neither the British nor the Soviet Government ever cancelled a major manifestation, with one exception: the Red Army Ensemble. When the Red Army invaded Czechoslovakia in 1968, the British Government announced that they couldn't come here when they were marching [into Prague]. I have a photograph for an advert for the concert at the Royal Albert Hall and someone wrote 'Now appearing in Prague' across it.

On the day of the Russian invasion of Prague, Russian cellist and conductor Mstislav Rostropovich was conducting a Dvořák concerto at the Hall, and the Hochhausers were expecting protests. 'The Head of the BBC, Sir William Glock, was expecting an enormous outburst and demonstration,' said Hochhauser.

Classical

'It was obviously overwhelming. It was the only hall of this particular size that accommodated five or six thousand people, which was very important for popular concerts. It was of course the only concert hall at this time where all the Promenade concerts took place and other major musical events presented by Harold Holt and now by myself. Of course, it was extremely impressive – particularly as you could see the stage from practically every angle. It was an enormous Hall with enormous facilities and it was at the same time intimate enough to accommodate concerts which people could enjoy without microphones.'

VICTOR HOCHHAUSER, TALKING ABOUT HIS FIRST IMPRESSIONS OF THE ROYAL ALBERT HALL

'But all that happened was that someone shouted out "Viva Casals!", and Rostropovich said, "Yes I agree – Viva Casals."' Lilian Hochhauser remembered: 'We were worried that he would be attacked. It was very, very tense. It was very emotional. It was one of the great moments of the Albert Hall.'

The legendary impresario – whose 'Victor Hochhauser Presents' tag became a byword for entertainment – also broke new ground by bringing the first ice ballet to the Royal Albert Hall – John Curry's *Symphony on Ice* in 1984 – and by arranging exchange visits between Russian and British orchestras in the 1980s and 1990s.

66. CLASSICAL MEETS ROCK

Deep Purple's founder and keyboard player Jon Lord, a talented composer, had long held an ambition to write a concerto for the group that could be performed with a full orchestra. On 24 September 1969, that dream came true when Deep Purple and the Royal Philharmonic Orchestra came together in the world's first fusion of rock and classical music, When Two Worlds Meet, in aid of the charity Task Force. Not everyone in the band was a fan of the idea, as guitarist Ritchie Blackmore later revealed:

I was not into classical music then. I was very, very moody and just wanted to play very loudly and jump around a lot. I couldn't believe we were playing with orchestras. We kept getting lumbered playing with them. We started off in '68 – this is my opinion – as a relatively competent band with a lot to say but saying it all at the same time as each other. In '69 we went into the classical stuff because it was Jon Lord's big thing to write a concerto for group and orchestra. He was very sincere. But I didn't like playing it or respect the fact that we were doing it. The orchestra was very condescending towards us, and I didn't like playing with them, so it was one big calamity on stage. But Jon was happy with it and management was happy with it. In 1970 I said, 'Right, we're going to make a rock 'n' roll LP. If this doesn't succeed I'll play in orchestras for the rest of my life,' because Jon wasn't too into hard rock. Luckily it took off, so I didn't have to play with orchestras anymore.

Despite his misgivings, the *Concerto For Group and Orchestra*, conducted by Malcolm Arnold and consisting of three movements, was a huge hit with the audience, as the *International Times* reported:

The group performed it magnificently, Blackmore demonstrating a dexterity that left some of the RPO string players gawking and the rest of the group playing to the best of their very substantial abilities. The standing ovation lasted about six minutes and clearly overwhelmed the group, particularly Jon, the author of the work. They played the last movement again and still found it difficult to leave the stage. The audience, which was a happy cross-section of the musical public, wouldn't let up. One realises why – the barriers are finally down.

67. A Brilliant Talent
Jacqueline du Pré, widely regarded as one of the best cellists of all time, performed at the Hall twelve times between 1962 and 1972. A child star, she was only seventeen years old when she appeared at the Proms for the first time. She often performed alongside her conductor husband, Daniel Barenboim, and her final performance at the Hall saw the pair headlining together. The career of the gifted musician was tragically cut short by the progress of multiple sclerosis, which forced her to stop performing at twenty-eight. She died in 1987, at the age of forty-two.

68. Pulling Strings
The violin has often taken centre stage at the Hall, with celebrity violinist Julian Lloyd Webber performing forty-one times. He first played at the Hall in 1976 as a young man of twenty-five, while still a student at the Royal College of Music. He also appeared at the Prince Philip, the Duke of Edinburgh's eightieth-birthday celebration in 2001, along with the celebrated harmonica player Larry Adler. At the BBC Children in Need Rocks the Royal Albert Hall concert in 2009, he appeared alongside Dizzee Rascal, Annie Lennox and Robbie Williams.

Nigel Kennedy, who first appeared at a Prom on 18 August 1981, is a huge

favourite at the Hall with classical and rock audiences alike. In November 2000, he appeared with the Who at a Teenage Cancer Trust concert, when he played 'Baba O'Riley'. In total, he has played at the Hall on twenty-four occasions including, in 2019, A Night at Ronnie Scott's: Sixtieth Anniversary Gala, alongside other stars such as Imelda May, Courtney Pine and Van Morrison.

Violin sensation Vanessa Mae brought her Red Hot Tour to the Albert Hall on 30 June 1995. The twenty-seven-year-old, who had been playing the instrument since she was three, rocked the audience with her 'violin techno-acoustic fusion' style, serving up high-speed renditions of everything from Johann Sebastian Bach's *Toccata and Fugue in D Minor* to Rednex's 'Cotton-Eye Joe', the latter accompanied by vocalist Kiki Dee. The concert was filmed for a bestselling DVD.

Another violinist to make a huge impact at the Hall is Nicola Benedetti, who made her debut at the Classical BRIT Awards on 25 May 2005, at the age of just seventeen. In 2012, the award-winning musician played the Last Night of the Proms, and a year later she sold out the whole venue in her own right, returning to headline again in 2013 and 2015.

In 2017, the Kanneh-Mason Trio headlined at the Hall. The group consists of the siblings Isata, who plays piano, violinist Braimah and cellist Sheku, who was the first black musician to win the BBC Young Musician of the Year award, in 2016. The trio were semi-finalists on *Britain's Got Talent* in 2015, and Sheku also performed at the wedding of Prince Harry and Meghan Markle in May 2018.

69. CLASSICAL SPECTACULAR

Over thirty years ago, music promoter Raymond Gubbay had the idea of combining classical music with special effects, such as lighting and lasers, to create a unique concert experience. The Classical Spectacular debuted at the Hall on 8 October 1989, featuring the Bands of the Scots and Welsh Guards, the musketeers of the Sealed Knot re-enactment society, and the Royal Philharmonic Orchestra. The programme contained such crowd-pleasers as Maurice Ravel's *Boléro*, Gioachino Rossini's 'William Tell Overture' and the duet from Georges Bizet's *The Pearl Fishers*.

Now an annual event, the show has played to an audience in excess of two million people in arenas throughout the UK, Europe and Australia, and there are twelve sold-out performances each year at the Hall. The programme changes each year but always includes Elgar's 'Land of Hope and Glory' and Tchaikovsky's *1812 Overture*. The music is accompanied by dancers, light shows, gunfire, lasers and fireworks, reflecting the mood of each piece. According to Gubbay:

> The idea was to make it as big and as brash as we could. We didn't have lasers originally but it was lights, the Guards' bands, the orchestra, the choir, the musketeers and using all of the Hall to its best advantage. I thought it was something that would work and it worked from day one. It's now settled down to two runs a year of six shows each and I'm very proud of that.

70. Hot Keys

Acclaimed Chinese pianist Lang Lang made his Hall debut at the BBC Proms in 2001, prompting *The Times* to write, 'Lang Lang took a sold-out Royal Albert Hall by storm ... This could well be history in the making.' Eight years later, after a blistering rendition of George Gershwin's *Rhapsody in Blue* at the 50th Annual Grammy Awards in Los Angeles the previous year, Lang Lang and Herbie Hancock repeated the key-duelling performance at the Hall, adding Ralph Vaughan-Williams' *Concerto for Two Pianos and Orchestra*, and a solo, duo and four-hand repertoire for piano, accompanied by the Philharmonia Orchestra and conducted by John Axelrod.

Since then, Lang Lang has headlined at the Hall on eleven occasions, including a special matinee concert for children and young adults on 17 April 2016, as part of the Hall's Education & Outreach programme. 'I want every child to have access to music experiences that ignite something wonderful inside of them, just as music delivered something incredible for me,' he said.

71. A Love Story

Today, the Hall hosts an annual twelve-day event celebrating classical music across all the different spaces that are available, from the auditorium to the underground loading bay to the Elgar Room. The Love Classical Festival started in March 2017, and comprised twenty-one events featuring such contributors as violinist Nigel Kennedy, pianist Lang Lang and trumpet player Alison Balsom. The London Contemporary Orchestra played in the loading bay; film-maker Christopher Nupen introduced a screening of his 1969 film, *The Trout*; and there was even a yoga session to live music.

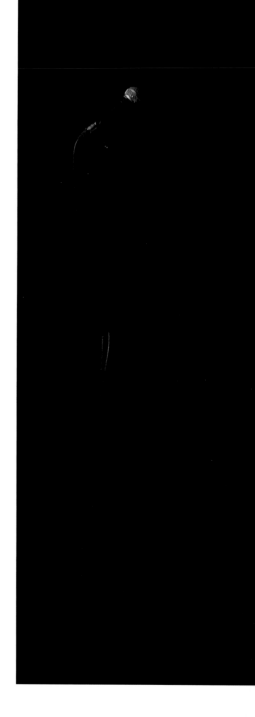

Stonewall
WORKING FOR LESBIAN AND GAY EQUALITY

ELTON JOHN STING ALISON MOYET

SHEBOOM, LILY SAVAGE & FRIENDS

1994 EQUALITY SHOW

SUNDAY 23RD OCTOBER 8PM

ROYAL ALBERT HALL WITH THANKS TO *ABSOLUT VODKA* FOR THEIR SUPPORT

7 SOCIAL & SCIENCE

Once dubbed the 'Nation's Village Hall', and 'available to hire' for one and all for any reasonable purpose, the Royal Albert Hall has seen an eclectic mix of characters and organisations pour through the doors. Following Prince Albert's vision of charitable outreach and inclusion, it has hosted religious groups, social groups and fundraising events throughout history, as well as presenting scientific demonstrations in line with the original intent.

'Albert's idea was a forum for the democratisation of science and learning,' says the Hall's CEO Craig Hassall. 'It was not a place for telling you stuff, but a place to share ideas and that's why it was designed as an oval building, not in a regular concert-hall shape. It became a place for meetings, conferences, protests and marches because you can have a lot more impact if you're screaming and ranting in this building than if you're in a town hall.'

72. MORSE APPARATUS DEMO
The use of the Hall for the arts and sciences was displayed early on with a fascinating demonstration of a 'modern ink-writing Morse apparatus, linked direct via Persia with Kurrachee [Karachi], 5,000 miles away' on 18 July 1872. The Society of Telegraph Engineers used a newly laid line to communicate with an operator in the distant city as the audience sat transfixed. First, the small apparatus produced the words 'Here, Kurrachee', prompting a similar response from the operator on the stage. The machine then clicked out the cryptic message 'The locusts are swarming in Scinde'. After that, the state-of-the-art contraption was used by the Grand Vizier of Persia to send a goodwill message to the Prince of Wales.

A demonstration of innovative new electrical-relay technology took place in

OPPOSITE: Handbill from Stonewall – 1994 Equality Show, 23 October 1994.

"THE COMING RACE" AT THE ALBERT HALL

BAZAAR FOR THE BENEFIT OF THE WEST END HOSPITAL, AND THE SCHOOL OF MASSAGE AND ELECTRICITY

1927, when over 6,000 Freemasons watched a dummy foundation stone being laid in the centre of the auditorium by the Grand Master of the United Grand Lodge of England – Prince Arthur, Duke of Connaught and Strathearn – to coincide with the real one being laid at the new Freemasons' Hall in Holborn. The dummy stone was lowered into place in three movements, accompanied by trumpet fanfares, and as it came to rest a green light, delivered by an electrical connection, confirmed that the actual foundation stone had been laid simultaneously.

73. Birth of the Sci-fi Convention

While Comic Cons and Star Trek conventions are now familiar events, the world's first sci-fi convention was actually held at the Royal Albert Hall between the fifth and tenth of March 1891. The theme was the bestselling 1871 novel *The Coming Race* by Edward Bulwer-Lytton, in which the Earth is threatened by the superior winged race called the 'Vril-ya'.

Those attending the convention were asked to come in fancy dress, and many came as the book's characters, including one young lady who dressed as Princess Zee with a black satin dress and a silver flower tiara that glowed with electric lights. Taking its lead from the author, who described Vril-ya architecture as being reminiscent of ancient Egypt, Sumer and India, the Hall was bedecked in flowers and palm leaves, and a grand 'Pillar of the Vril-ya', modelled on Cleopatra's Needle, formed the centrepiece. Grand banquets were held and sci-fi fans were entertained by Vril-themed magic shows, a fortune-telling dog and musical acts, while winged Vril-ya mannequins flew above.

74. All Dolled Up

The striking sight of thousands of dolls arranged in towering pyramids stretching across the auditorium could be the stuff of nightmares for some, but for poor children in Victorian London, it was a Christmas wish come true. The annual Truth Doll and Toy Show, which ran for twenty years from 1892, transformed the Hall into a child's paradise for two days in the festive period.

Each year, around 30,000 children in hospitals, workhouses, workhouse schools, orphanages and Poor Law schools received a small gift of a doll or toy, while larger and more expensive gifts, such as dolls' houses, forts and Noah's Arks were handed to the institutions for children to share. Tom Smith – the firm that invented the Christmas cracker – provided 25,000 of its products, while 11,000 new sixpences were donated by copper-magnate Francis Tress Barry for the older children.

The charitable event was organised by Henry Labouchère, editor of society

The Great "Truth" Doll Show : *At the Royal Albert Hall.*

THE MADONNA
In "The Miracle"

Rose in "Trelawney of the Wells," dressed by Miss Irene Vanbrugh;
Elizabeth Sydenham in "Drake," dressed by Miss Amy Brandon
Thomas; and Imogen Parrott in "Trelawney of the Wells," dressed by
Miss Fay Davis

Our congratulations to Mr. R. A. Bennett, the editor of "Truth,"
on the fact that that journal has suffered nothing in prestige or in
popularity since it lost Mr. Labouchere and Mr. Voules. This fact
is brought out in the most striking manner by the success of the
"Truth" Doll Show at the Albert Hall, to which her Majesty the
Queen contributed a national group of three dolls entitled Rose,
Shamrock, and Thistle. This show has been annually organised
by "Truth" for thirty-three years, and the dolls and toys collected
from a thousand quarters are distributed at Christmas among the
children in workhouses, schools, infirmaries, and voluntary hospitals in
London. By means of this noble charity more than 30,000 poor
children receive a Christmas present every year—a doll or a toy.
A great feature of the toys this year were popular actresses in
well-known parts, for which Lady Tree dressed a doll representing Mrs.
Patrick Campbell in her part in "Bel'a Donna."

THE NUN
In "The Miracle"

Between 1896 and 1925, audiences didn't even need to be in the Royal Albert Hall to hear a concert or speech. In keeping with the Hall's remit to advance the sciences, the Electrophone Company operated an innovative system that permitted subscribers to dial in using a telephone-like device to listen to events at the Hall, echo and all. Transmitters at the front of the stage allowed the sound to travel through underground and overground wires to the receivers in the user's home – these were similar in shape to the modern headphone and, according to the journal *The Electrical Engineer* in 1897, were 'conveniently arranged on a light metal frame'.

'A small flat table of polished wood is provided to carry the contact jacks,' the report continued. 'This can be stood on a convenient table and connected with the system by a wall socket and plug and a length of twin cord. The receivers are for an ordinary subscriber four in number, but extra ones can be fitted if desired.' The service wasn't cheap. Subscription cost £50 a year – around £5,600 in today's money.

journal *Truth*, and 4,000 of the dolls were dressed by its readers – some managed to dress over four hundred each. The readers' imaginations knew no bounds, coming up with costumes that ranged from queens of England or Cinderella, to national dresses or scenes from *Pride and Prejudice* and *A Midsummer Night's Dream*. Famous actresses even sent replicas of their favourite stage costumes.

In the last few years of the show, Queen Mary presented groups of dolls representing different themes, such as a wedding and a nursery, for the girls, while providing soldiers, sailors, lions, tigers and rocking horses for the boys.

75. A Sound Revolution

The first ever gramophone concert at the Hall was held on 14 December 1906, and mixed live performances with recordings from popular opera singers such as Adelina Patti, Dame Nellie Melba and the Italian tenor Enrico Caruso.

The event was essentially a sales pitch for the Auxeto Gramophone Company, so the tickets were free – all 9,000 were snapped up in twenty-four hours. Music was played on the Auxetophone Sound Box, invented by Horace Short and Charles Parsons, the latter of whom also perfected the steam turbine. The ingenious contraption used air pressure to increase the volume and push sound out to all parts of the auditorium and, at one point, its power was demonstrated with an unexpected twist. After a performance by soprano Amy Castles, the audience called enthusiastically for an encore. Instead of stepping forward to reprise the song, Castles stepped back and the audience listened to her 'encore', the same piece, played on a plastic record on the gramophone. Although impressive, the Auxetophone, later manufactured by the American firm Victor, was not intended for home use and few were sold, not least because of the hefty price tag of around £100 (equivalent to £10,500 today).

In a more recent demonstration of the fusion of music and science, the American rapper Will.i.am showcased his latest tech venture – a smartwatch called 'dial' – at the 2017 Black Eyed Peas reunion gig. The star performed his hit 'Scream and Shout', with the watch's voice assistant taking the role of Britney Spears .

76. Dr Macaura and the Pulsocon

'Doctor' Gerald Joseph Macaura was an Irish man who travelled to London in the early 1900s to promote his hand-held vibrator which, he claimed, cured a multitude of ills. Macaura's Pulsocon (later Macaura's Blood Circulator) had a vibrating plate that was placed over the ailing body part and, when the handle was turned, passed a strong vibration through the skin, curing – he claimed

– nervous disorders, pain, deafness, anaemia, heart disease, cramp, polio and 'women's problems'.

As his fame grew, he staged several demonstrations of the instrument at the Royal Albert Hall on 19 and 30 April 1910, and again on 11 May 1911. As well as a lecture and practical demonstration, these evenings promised 'Mr W.T. Stead's formerly crippled patients to publicly testify and tell their own story of their cure'. Macaura's third show didn't quite go to plan, as it was gatecrashed by two hundred medical students, who heckled and jeered the 'doctor', before finally being told to be quiet by an audience member. *The Times* reported the ensuing scenes with evident amusement:

> Shortly afterwards the students began to leave the hall, but before doing so they burst a large number of bladders of foul gas in the building and strewed chemicals over the seats. The students then assembled outside the building and marched in procession to Knightsbridge, singing and cheering, with a coffin at their head. They passed along Piccadilly some two hundred strong, and were approaching Piccadilly Circus when two bodies of police charged them from opposite directions. For some minutes there was great disorder, but the police soon got the upper hand, captured the coffin, and broke up the demonstrators.

Although business continued to boom, Macaura was eventually exposed as a fraud and jailed for three years. Even so, versions of the Pulsocon continued to be sold right through to the 1950s. The archive at the Royal Albert Hall contains an original Pulsocon, though not the original one from the demonstrations at the Hall.

77. Shackleton's Doomed Adventure

One historic event at the Hall was a presentation in 1919 by Ernest Shackleton about his perilous expedition in the *Endurance* to the Antarctic. Five years earlier, on 8 August 1914, the renowned explorer had set off on the Imperial Trans-Antarctic Expedition, an attempt to cross the frozen continent via the South Pole. Two years later his ship, *Endurance*, became trapped in ice and sank, leaving all twenty-eight crewmembers stranded on Elephant Island. Shackleton and five of his crew launched the *James Caird* lifeboat and, battling horrendous conditions in the open boat, made an 800-mile (1,300-kilometre), four-week journey to the Atlantic island of South Georgia. There, he and two of his men made a perilous thirty-six-hour crossing through mountainous territory to reach the whaling station, where he could finally enlist some help to rescue the rest of his crew.

On its return to England, the 23-foot (7-metre) *James Caird* was put on display on the stage of the Royal Albert Hall and, on 19 December 1919, Shackleton stood in front of it to tell the story of his fateful expedition and to introduce an accompanying film in aid of the Middlesex Hospital. The lifeboat also went on display at Selfridges, and today can be found at a London boarding school, Dulwich College.

While all twenty-eight crew members returned to the UK safely, there was a tragic twist in the tale, as they arrived home in the midst of the First World

RIGHT: Sir Ernest Shackleton showed moving pictures and shared the amazing story of his Antarctic expedition at the Hall on 19 December 1919.

Social & Science

War. As *The Times* noted in its review of the evening at the Hall, 'most of them volunteered for active service, and on the screen one sees men who subsequently gave their lives for their country – one killed with his gun in the Channel, another drowned while mine-sweeping.'

78. LIFE SAVERS

In the aftermath of the First World War, a blockade stopping food and medicine getting to German and Austrian cities stayed in place. Families in once wealthy cities such as Berlin and Vienna were starving, and millions of children were left malnourished and suffering from rickets. In 1919, two British sisters, Eglantyne Jebb and Dorothy Buxton, helped found the Fight the Famine movement to confront the situation, distributing leaflets in Trafalgar Square showing shocking pictures of emaciated children under the headline: 'Our Blockade has caused this – millions of children are starving to death'. Jebb was arrested for her protest and found guilty, but the prosecuting counsel was so impressed by her passion for the cause that he offered to pay the £5 fine himself. This was to be the first donation to the Save the Children Fund, which the sisters launched at a packed public meeting of sympathisers at the Royal Albert Hall that May.

Over the following months and years, the Fund raised considerable amounts for organisations working to feed and educate children in Germany, Austria, France, Belgium, Hungary and the Balkans, as well as for Armenian refugees in Turkey. When Russia was hit by famine in 1921, they took out full-page adverts in the papers and showed disturbing footage in cinemas of children living in substandard conditions. This time, instead of handing the cash to other aid funds, Jebb and her co-workers filled a ship with six hundred tons of aid and sent it to Russia. Through the winter of 1921 and much of 1922, daily meals provided by Save the Children helped to keep 300,000 children and more than 350,000 adults alive – for a shilling per person per week.

By the time she died in 1928, Jebb had established Save the Children as both an effective relief agency, able to provide food, clothing and money to those in need, and also a political organisation, fighting for children's rights both in the UK and globally. Just a year before her death, she said of her charity: 'It must not be content to save children from the hardships of life – it must abolish these hardships; nor think it suffices to save them from immediate menace – it must place in their hands the means of saving themselves and so of saving the world.'

In the one hundred years since Save the Children was established, the Royal Albert Hall has been instrumental in raising millions for the fund, with regular charity events including carol concerts, a biennial fête and, in 1984, the Dinner at Albert's event in aid of starving children in Ethiopia. In May 2019, a bronze bust of Eglantyne Jebb by the artist Ian Wolter was unveiled at the Hall to mark the centenary of the charity, and it is now on display at the charity's Farringdon headquarters.

79. LEST WE FORGET

The First World War claimed the lives 886,000 British service personnel, and left 1.6 million wounded. Five years after the final shot was fired, the first

Festival of Remembrance – now an annual event – was held at the Royal Albert Hall on 11 November 1923. Entitled 'In Memory 1914–1918: A Cenotaph In Sound', the concert was in aid of Field-Marshal Earl Haig's Appeal for Ex-Service Men of all Ranks, better known as the Royal British Legion. The Prince of Wales, later Edward VIII, was in the King's Box to hear an ambitious new composition by the British composer John Foulds, *A World Requiem: A Cenotaph in Sound*, performed by a chorus and orchestra, which was to be performed at the annual concert until 1926. That year, the concert was renamed the Festival of Remembrance, and began featuring morale-boosting wartime songs such as 'Pack up Your Troubles', 'Take Me Back to Dear Old Blighty' and 'It's a Long Way to Tipperary'. The event ended with the now familiar service, featuring 'The Last Post' and concluding with the National Anthem.

In 1928, George V was the first monarch to attend. The stage was built into the structure of a dugout, with a Union Jack stretched over the ceiling, while the main gangway leading to the platform became a trench. No Remembrance Festival took place during the early years of the Second World War, but in 1945 the event was transformed into the ceremony that we would recognise today, with patriotic and popular songs, alongside the religious service and the stirring procession of the armed services and support organisations. The year also marked the start of having two separate festivals, one for the Royal Family and invited guests, and one open to the public. Millions more were able to watch the proceedings when it was first televised in 1950.

The Queen first visited the Hall as Patron for the Festival of Remembrance on 8 November 1952, aged just twenty-six. She still frequently attends the event, necessitating the use of the hammercloth, which is draped over the front of the Queen's Box for the monarch's visit.

The Royal British Legion Festival of Remembrance continues to commemorate those lost in both World Wars and subsequent conflicts, including Afghanistan and Iraq. The two performances, in the afternoon and evening, feature marching drills and manoeuvres, as well as music and performances, culminating in a drop of poppy petals from the roof and a two-minute silence.

Since 2001, the event has featured popular singers such as Bryn Terfel, Katherine Jenkins, Russell Watson, Jamie Cullum, Alfie Boe, Cliff Richard, Pixie Lott, Tom Odell, Gregory Porter and Tom Jones. In 2014, the actors and cast of the National Theatre's *War Horse* put on the *War Horse Prom*, featuring the original puppets and Michael Morpurgo narrating a new War Horse Suite, composed by Adrian Sutton from his score for the original production.

BRITISH LEGION

Patron : HIS MAJESTY THE KING.
President : MAJOR-GENERAL SIR F. MAURICE, K.C.M.G., C.B.
Chairman : BRIGADIER-GENERAL E. R. FITZPATRICK, C.B.E., D.S.O., D.L.
Vice-Chairman : LIEUT.-COLONEL SIR IAN FRASER, C.B.E., M.P.
Hon. Treasurer : MAJOR SIR BRUNEL COHEN.   *General Secretary :* J. R. GRIFFIN.

FESTIVAL *of* SERVICE *and* REMEMBRANCE
ROYAL ALBERT HALL
(*Manager :* MR. C. S. TAYLOR.)
Saturday, November 11th, 1944, at 2.30 and 7 p.m.

MASSED BANDS
of the Scots Guards and the Irish Guards
Conductor : CAPTAIN G. H. WILLCOCKS, M.B.E., A.R.C.M., P.S.M.
TRUMPETERS OF THE ROYAL MILITARY SCHOOL OF MUSIC
(*By kind permission of the Commandant*).

Organ : DR. O. M. PEASGOOD, MUS. D., Organist of Westminster Abbey.
FLIGHT-SERGEANT LIONEL SMITH.

Directors of Music :
SCOTS GUARDS : CAPTAIN S. RHODES, MUS. BAC., A.R.C.M., P.S.M.
IRISH GUARDS : CAPTAIN G. H. WILLCOCKS, M.B.E., A.R.C.M., P.S.M.
ROYAL MARINES : CAPTAIN F. VIVIAN DUNN, M.V.O., A.R.A.M.
ROYAL MILITARY SCHOOL OF MUSIC : LIEUTENANT M. ROBERTS, L.R.A.M., A.R.C.M., P.S.M.

Organiser : J. R. GRIFFIN.
Producer : **Squadron Leader RALPH READER, M.B.E.**
Assistant Producers : FLIGHT-LIEUTENANT CRACKNELL, W.O.'s BEET, CAMERON, HEALY and
AC. ALBERT LOCK.
Narrator : HENRY OSCAR.

OVERLEAF: Royal British
Legion's Festival of
Remembrance,
8 November 2008.

80. HAPPY CAMPERS

Butlin's holiday camps were converted for military use during the Second World
War, but they enjoyed a post-war boom with families snapping up a week of
sea, sand and entertainment for the price of a weekly pay packet. From 1946,
holidaymakers could relive their happy memories at the annual Butlin's Reunion
Festival at the Hall, featuring music from various orchestras, including the
Butlin Concert Orchestra, and star turns from the likes of the Beverley Sisters.
Holidaymakers and Redcoats mingled on the dance floor at the packed event,
which also included table-tennis and billiard demonstrations. Winners of the

bathing-beauty competitions from each camp came together for a grand final, with the victor being crowned Butlin's Holiday Princess.

The highlight of the events, which ran for anything from two to five days in February, was the appearance of Prince Philip, Duke of Edinburgh, with company founder Billy Butlin. The Redcoats formed a guard of honour to welcome the pair, before Philip was presented with a cheque for the National Playing Fields Association, and he then responded with a well-received speech.

81. YOUTH MOVEMENT

The Methodist Association of Youth Clubs (MAYC) was formally launched at the Hall on 2 June 1945, following a meeting at Westminster Central Hall addressed by the Labour MP Stafford Cripps. Led by the head of the Church's youth department, Douglas Griffiths, the 'launching of the good ship' featured music from the Boys' Brigade Band and hymns, before the official launching ceremony. The new group was organised along inclusive, non-paternal principles, encouraging the participation of young members of the Methodist Church, and eventually led to the establishment of the MAYC National Members Council in 1966, which endorsed the inclusion of young people in the leadership of the movement at every level.

Following the launch event, the MAYC returned to the Hall annually as part of its London Weekend, enjoying an evening of hymns, speeches and displays of skills including dance and theatre. The event became so popular that by the 1950s a second evening had been added, bringing the total number of young members attending to 12,500. The meetings continued until 1998.

82. COOKING WITH GAS

Today celebrity chefs are everywhere, but in the 1950s there was really only one household name in the business – Fanny Cradock. Famous for her no-nonsense style, extravagant evening gowns and clipped tones, Cradock and her husband Johnnie already had a successful television show when they appeared at the Hall on 12 and 13 December 1956 to present their show Bon Viveur. The evening was a tribute to Fanny's great hero, French chef Georges Auguste Escoffier, with dishes including onion soup and honey-roasted goose. At one point, Cradock recreated Escoffier's Peach Melba dessert – named in honour of Royal Albert Hall regular Dame Nellie Melba – presenting it on the back of a huge ice sculpture of a swan, just as Escoffier's original had been.

In typically flamboyant style, Cradock walked onto the stage in a white fur stole, which she then shed to reveal a stylish taffeta ball gown and diamond jewellery, while Johnnie wore full evening dress. During the interval, the centre of the auditorium was transformed into a bistro where a lucky few could taste the feast, while the couple adopted the personas of a French wife and her cockney husband, with Cradock running through her recipes in a French accent, and Johnnie wearing a striped T-shirt and beret. Sponsored by the Gas Council, and featuring its mascot Mr Therm, the show also included a segment in which Johnnie almost ruined the soufflé by forgetting to turn the oven on, but Cradock cooked it on a higher heat then declared, 'You see, you can't go wrong with gas.'

83. A Cultural Revolution

The birth of the 1960s counterculture movement can, for many involved, be traced back to one event. 'In Britain you could date the emergence of the underground to 11 June 1965, the day of the International Poetry Incarnation at the Royal Albert Hall,' said writer and leading light Barry Miles. 'The audience looked at each other and realised they were a community. From that meeting underground papers were born, as were numerous art galleries, boutiques, friendships and relationships.'

Considered one of the first British 'happenings' of the hippie movement, the event saw around 7,000 pack into the Hall to hear Beat legend Allen Ginsberg read 'New York Bird' by Russian poet Andrei Voznesensky – who was in the building but forbidden to perform by the Soviet authorities – as well as his own poems 'The Change' and 'Who Be Kind To'. Other readers included Lawrence Ferlinghetti, Gregory Corso, Adrian Mitchell and Michael Horovitz.

The crowd were heavy drinkers and the Hall soon filled with marijuana smoke and paper planes. Flowers were handed out on the way in, and they too were thrown, dropped and strewn all over the stage. A few years later, artist, poet and musician Jeff Nuttall described the scene, writing 'separate audiences had come to one place at the same time, to witness an atmosphere of pot, impromptu solo acid dances, of incredible barbaric colour, of face and body painting, of flowers and flowers and flowers, of a common dreaminess in which all was permissive and benign.' While the event proved a pivotal point in the hippie movement in Britain, the Hall's manager was not impressed, complaining 'I don't want that sort of filth here. Would you send your teenage daughter to hear that sort of thing?'

Nonetheless, the anniversary of the event saw a second invasion the following year for the New Moon Carnival in the Round. This time, the poetry headliners were British stars including Robert Graves, Stevie Smith, Michael Horovitz, Spike Milligan and Vanessa Redgrave. This time, the Hall's manager reported that 'the event broke up in complete disorder, but not before bottles, glasses, ashtrays, potted plants, flowers and greenery had been hurled across the arena.' He also alleged that a ten-gallon drum of paraffin oil and thirty home-made torches soaked in paraffin were discovered in the basement. The latter claim was not fully investigated, but the Hall's Council were worried enough to rule that 'no further bookings of this kind should be accepted in the future', and poetry events were banned for eighteen years.

84. INSTANT KARMA

The Royal Albert Hall also witnessed the birth of 'Bagism', John Lennon and Yoko Ono's satirical protest against prejudice. In December 1968, an alternative arts centre, the Arts Lab, organised an underground Christmas party, The Celebration, with appearances by *One Flew Over the Cuckoo's Nest* author Ken Kesey, the California Hells Angels, the Third Ear Band and chanting by Hare Krishna devotees. During the evening, John and Yoko performed their *Alchemical Wedding*, climbing into a white cloth bag, and staying there while a musician played a flute for thirty minutes. The couple started sitting cross-legged and moved twice, in order to lie closer to the floor.

John and Yoko's performance art wasn't the only notable event at The Celebration. When audience member Elizabeth Marsh stripped naked and a steward attempted to cover her up, other concert-goers began to show their solidarity by stripping too. 'A young girl stripped and sat naked in her seat during a pop concert at the Albert Hall last night,' reported *The Times*. 'When police tried to get near the girl, other members of the audience started to take off their clothes. One man stood naked for a while. Police officers and hall officials were jeered, booed and clapped. The girl later put her coat round her shoulders ... After the girl had covered herself the concert continued with some quiet Indian music.'

Former crew manager Martin O'Gorman remembers the occasion well:

It was a hippy night. Unbelievable it was. There was this young girl who was right at the bottom of G stalls. She started stripping off, naked, and this bloke came down and said, 'Come on madam you've got to leave.' All of a sudden everyone started stripping off. Everybody! So what do you do now? Can't get

them all out. Then Yoko and John got on the stage and I was watching and the two of them in the sack rolling across the stage. [Later] I picked up that sack and I threw it in the bin. I could have held on to it. God knows what I would have got for it!

The superstar couple carried on their Bagism protests over the next year, famously inviting journalists to a press conference in Vienna then refusing to leave the bag they were in, claiming that not allowing the press to judge them on their physical appearance led to 'total communication with no prejudice'.

85. A SPIRITUAL FORCE

After an exhaustive tour of the UK during which he held three-day workshops in Buddhist teachings, His Holiness the Dalai Lama, Tenzin Gyatso, made his first speech at the Hall on 5 July 1984, accompanied by the Dean of Westminster, Edward Carpenter. Speaking to a packed house, the exiled Tibetan leader expounded on the theme of peace, and stated that one thing unites all humanity: 'All beings want to be happy. They want to avoid pain and suffering.'

Following his sell-out speech, the Dalai Lama, who is now the longest-lived incumbent of the post and won the Nobel Peace Prize in 1989, returned three more times, in 1999, 2008 and 2012. During his last visit, he examined the relationship between heart and mind, and how best to develop an open heart, telling the audience: 'Think more, analyse more, experiment, examine the evidence. From conviction comes enthusiasm to implement, then real effect comes.' Technical projects manager Stephanie Baldwin remembers a secret message that he had for the Hall's team: 'I lit the show and I was told if the lights are getting a bit too bright, he will put on a tennis visor,' she says. 'Sure enough, halfway through the event, he put the hat on. That was my cue to gently reduce the lights a bit.'

The Hall has seen diverse celebrations across many religions and philosophies over the years. An early multicultural event was the Anglo-Jewish Exhibition, which ran from 4 April to 2 July 1887, showcasing manuscripts and other antiquities significant to Jewish culture. Exhibits included documents, pictures, prints, books, a model of a temple, a tabernacle, maps, autographs, coins, scrolls and music. In 1920, Arthur Balfour led the speeches in the Hall at a celebration of the granting of a mandate for Palestine to Britain, which accepted the need for a 'national home for Jewish people' in the region in the wake of the First World War. In April 1968, the twentieth anniversary of Israel's Independence Day was celebrated at the Hall, with performers including Roger Moore, Ron Moody, David Jacobs and Diana Coupland.

In 1976, two musical performances featuring choirs and singers from Pakistan formed part of the World of Islam Festival. The Festival was opened by the Queen and ran until June 1976, aiming to foster a deeper understanding of Islamic civilisation through its art, geography, philosophy, literature and religion.

The venue also celebrated the 300th birthdays of Guru Gobind Singh, the tenth Sikh Guru, on 27 January 1967, and the soldier-saints the Khalsa Panth on 25 April 1999; and the 400th anniversary of the first reading of the religious scripture Sri Guru Granth Sahib Ji on 26 September 2004.

86. BRIT OF A SHAMBLES
The Brit Awards have twice been held in the Hall, in 1988 and 1989, with both editions broadcast live on television. The first, hosted by Noel Edmonds, featured the last live performance from Banararama before Siobhan Fahey left the group, and the last performance by the Who with Kenney Jones as a member. It also featured a memorable duet, when the Pet Shop Boys debuted their collaboration

For one week every year the Hall is transformed into an elegant dining venue for corporate events. The Exhibition Floor is put in and tables and chairs are dotted across the arena. Tables of five or eight can also be fitted into the boxes. In-house caterers Rhubarb then serve a three-course meal to 2,000 diners every night:

134 tables

2,000 covers

One main production kitchen
Seven satellite kitchens across the building

20 to 24 chefs work in the main kitchen, which also produces meals for the staff

60 staff in satellite kitchens

Every kitchen is colour-coded, and the staff wear different uniforms to identify their jobs and use radios to communicate

with Dusty Springfield on 'What Have I Done to Deserve This?'

But it was the 1989 Brits that proved notorious, making headlines for all the wrong reasons. Presenters Mick Fleetwood and Samantha Fox fluffed their lines, left awkward silences and were frequently drowned out by the screams of the Bros fans, known as 'Brosettes'. At six foot five inches, Fleetwood towered over Fox, who stood just five foot one inch tall, a height difference that didn't help the chemistry. On top of these issues, the autocue jammed and guests showed up on stage at the wrong time, with Fox introducing the Four Tops, only to have Boy George walk on stage. The pair also forgot to announce the nominees for best newcomer altogether, leaving presenters Ronnie Wood and Bill Wyman standing on the stage looking confused.

Sam Fox, who was just nineteen at the time, later admitted, 'When everything started going wrong I just wanted the floor to swallow me up.' Because of the debacle, dubbed 'the worst Brits ever' in the press, the awards ceremony was pre-recorded the following year, and wasn't broadcast live for another eighteen years.

87. Dropping a Clanger

Banquets and huge dinners have been a regular feature at the Hall, but perhaps the most memorable was a conference held by the Institute of Directors on 23 April 1991. After-dinner speaker Gerald Ratner livened up the business banquet by telling guests that his Ratners jewellery chain was selling cut-glass sherry decanters complete with six glasses on a silver-plated tray for £4.95. He went on to relate how, when asked how he could sell the set at such a low price, he had responded, 'Because it's total crap.' He made matters worse by telling the astonished crowd that he also sold a pair of earrings 'which is cheaper than a prawn sandwich from Marks & Spencer', adding, 'but I have to say that the sandwich will probably last longer than the earrings.'

The extraordinary speech instantly wiped £500 million from the company's share price and prompted his resignation. It also gave rise to the phrase 'doing a Ratner', meaning to reveal something which is probably true, but unwise to make public.

88. Black Holes fill the Albert Hall

On 22 November 1995, Stephen Hawking became the second physicist to fill the Hall, over sixty years after Albert Einstein had become the first. In fact, the 5,000 tickets were snapped up in five days after being advertised in *The Times*. The celebrated cosmologist, who became a household name after the release

Waterstone's presents
Stephen Hawking
at the Royal Albert Hall

On Wednesday, 22 November at 7.30pm Stephen Hawking, the legendary scientist and author of *A Brief History of Time*, will make a rare public appearance at the Royal Albert Hall to deliver a lecture entitled

"Does God Throw Dice in Black Holes?"

The evening will be introduced by J.P. McEvoy, author of *Stephen Hawking for Beginners*, and after the lecture both McEvoy and Hawking will take questions.

Tickets are available from 1 September from the Royal Albert Hall ticket office priced £10 and £12, concessions £7. Box office open 9.00am –9.00pm seven days a week. Credit card bookings on 0171–589 8212 (£2.50 transaction charge on all telephone and postal bookings).

WATERSTONE'S

ABOVE: Handbill from Professor Stephen Hawking Lecture – 'Does God Throw Dice in Black Holes?', 22 November 1995.

of his first book *A Brief History of Time*, refused a fee for the appearance and donated all funds to the Motor Neurone Disease Association. His speech, entitled 'Does God Throw Dice in Black Holes?', answered critics who had previously accused him of ignoring religious beliefs in his theories surrounding the birth of the universe. The title was a reference to Einstein's famous assertion that 'God does not play dice'. Hawking suggested that 'Consideration of black holes suggests, not only that God does play dice, but that he sometimes confuses us by throwing them where they can't be seen.' He ended the talk on a similar theme, stating: 'God still has a few tricks up his sleeve.'

The brilliant scientist, who had battled motor neurone disease since he was a Cambridge student, returned to the Hall again in October 2010 for the Professor Stephen Hawking Lecture. He talked about his childhood and his life, before moving on to the latest instalment in his 'Grand Unified Theory of Everything'. He explained the universe through a series of interlinked models, which he compared to maps with different scales that link up to show the whole picture. He then finished the talk by taking three questions, including, 'Do you think there will come a time when people will learn everything about physics?' to which he replied 'I hope not!'

Hawking's last appearance at the Hall was in 2015, at the world premiere of *Interstellar Live*, a screening of the science-fiction film *Interstellar* accompanied by a sixty-piece orchestra. He took to the stage to introduce a pre-screening talk with the film's director Christopher Nolan, the composer of its soundtrack, Hans Zimmer, and the physicist Kip Thorne, hosted by Brian Cox.

89. A GIG FOR EQUALITY
In 1988, the passing of Section 28 of the Local Government Act, which banned the 'promotion' of homosexuality, prompted the formation of protest group Stonewall. The British charity, which campaigns for LGBT rights, went from

strength to strength and, on 23 October 1994, the first of seven Stonewall Equality shows brought a host of famous names flocking to the stage at the Hall.

After a resounding opening from the sixty-strong female drumming band Sheboom, Paul O'Grady's alter ego Lily Savage took the stage, and was followed by performances from Sandi Toksvig, Alison Moyet and the Pet Shop Boys. Labour leader Tony Blair and his wife, the human-rights lawyer Cherie Blair, were in attendance, while the Hollywood actor Richard Gere got up on stage to quash rumours that he was gay by announcing that he was a lesbian.

The evening had a memorable finale, which was written up in the *Evening Standard* the following day:

> Sting almost brought the house down when he started a slow striptease in front of Elton [John] as they duetted on 'Big Spender'. It ended with a bare-chested Sting down to his leather trousers. Their double act, introduced by Neil Tennant and Chris Lowe of the Pet Shop Boys, was the climax to an evening that raised £100,000 for Stonewall.

Over the next seven years, the many stars who performed at the fundraising show included Kylie Minogue, Antonio Banderas, George Michael, Alison Moyet, Boy George, Gary Barlow, Judi Dench and Graham Norton.

90. A MAGICAL EVENING

The Royal Albert Hall was transformed into Hogwarts, complete with flying ghosts on 26 June 2003 for the launch of the book *Harry Potter and the Order of the Phoenix*. As thousands of fans across the country queued at bookshops to buy the fifth book in the bestselling series, 5,000 lucky schoolchildren were given free tickets to the event, at which they could quiz author J.K. Rowling about their favourite characters and plots, and hear her reading extracts from the latest instalment. Stephen Fry, who narrates the Harry Potter audiobooks, hosted the evening and the avid Potter fans, many dressed as witches and wizards, greeted J.K. Rowling with an enthusiasm described by *The Guardian* as 'close to Beatlemania'.

The first Hall event to be live-streamed on the internet, the book reading was in marked contrast to that of the first book, which, as Rowling told the audience, had been in front of just two people. Harry Potter has since returned to the Hall in cinema form, with a series of film concerts, at which the scores are played by the Royal Philharmonic Concert Orchestra.

91. Inspiring Women

When the Queen went to cut the fruitcake at the Women's Institute centenary celebrations in 2015, the knife got stuck, much to the amusement of Her Majesty and her companions Princess Anne and the Countess of Wessex. The cake was duly cut into bite-sized pieces to be handed out later as guests left the Hall. The Queen had earlier received the 'centenary baton' and been shown a film of its journey around Britain, before she declared the annual general meeting officially open.

For the thousands of women who thronged to the Hall, this meeting was a special one, celebrating one hundred years since the National Federation of Women's Institutes was formed and the first Women's Institute (WI) meeting in Great Britain held in the town of Llanfairpwll on Anglesey on 16 September 1915. Since then, the WI has grown to become the largest women's voluntary organisation in the UK with over 212,000 members in 6,600 groups.

The WI association with the Hall is a long one – over eighty events have been held at the venue since the first annual meeting in 19 May 1931. At that landmark meeting, led by Gertrude Denman, the attendees passed resolutions

OPPOSITE: J.K. Rowling's
'Harry Potter and the
Order of the Phoenix'
Book Launch at the Royal
Albert Hall, 26 June 2003.

RIGHT: WI members
having picnics during
the lunch break of the
Centenary meeting of the
WI at the Royal Albert
Hall attended by HM
Queen Elizabeth II,
4 June 2015.

calling for improved antenatal provision in rural areas, for hospital patients not to be woken before seven o'clock in the morning, for the extension of national marks safeguarding food standards to cover preserved fruit and vegetables, and for farmed fur to be produced humanely.

A letter to *The Times* on 23 May from one Christopher Turnor praised '[t]he great gathering at the Albert Hall' as 'a striking testimony to the growth and strength of that remarkable movement.' It added: 'The movement has brought a new interest into the lives of hundreds of thousands of country women; indeed, it is not too much to say that it has created a new spirit in our country life.'

In 1943, WI members were delighted by an unexpected visit from the president of the Sandringham branch – Queen Elizabeth – who wanted to thank them for their efforts 'towards the winning of this war':

Today, the place of the countrywoman is more important than it has ever been before. Despite all the wartime difficulties, it is she who must care for the workers who are growing our food, use her skill to make the best possible use of that food, bring up her children to love and defend those values for which we are fighting, and guide them to love and cherish the beautiful country of which we are so proud.

Queen Elizabeth the Queen Mother was also a staunch supporter of the WI, and was at the 1954 meeting at which a resolution was passed that led to the Keep Britain Tidy campaign against litter. Four years later, the 1958 Litter Act was passed and MPs thanked the National Federation of Women's Institutes for their input in litter policy.

In 2012, the National Federation broke the world record for the most people knitting together at the same time, with over 3,000 taking part in the Hall. WI member Lynne Stubbings, who took part in the challenge, recalled, 'It was all good fun, but slightly bizarre.' The annual general meeting is an all-day event, and passers-by are often amazed at the sight of 5,000 women congregating on the steps of the Albert Memorial and the surrounding grass to enjoy their packed lunches and flasks of tea.

92. Fashionable Place to Be

Princess Diana was the guest of honour at the first British Fashion Awards, held on 17 October 1989. The event, celebrating British designers, creatives and models on the international fashion scene, was billed as the largest and most lavish fashion show ever seen in London. Typically, designer of the year nominee Vivienne Westwood did nothing to spare royal blushes, presenting a transparent bodysuit with a fig-leaf-covered crotch, while Katharine Hamnett went a step further, displaying silver-studded leather G-strings. Diana showcased her own effortless style with an iconic white-beaded 'Elvis' dress and jacket, designed by Catherine Walker.

The British Fashion Awards were held at the Hall on a further three occasions, in 1990, 1996 and 1997. The event's successor, known simply as the Fashion Awards, has been held at the Hall since 2016 and has seen performances from the likes of Eric Clapton and Rita Ora, as well as appearances from a host of famous guests, including Steve McQueen, Lady Gaga, David and Victoria Beckham, Dina Asher-Smith, Katarina Johnson-Thompson, Kate Beckinsale, Kendall Jenner and Cate Blanchett. In 2019, a then pregnant Meghan Markle, Duchess of Sussex, was a special guest. Naomi Campbell gave an emotional speech that same year after becoming the first black woman to win the Fashion Icon award at the ceremony, calling it an 'out of body experience'.

Even before the awards, the Hall has had a long history of fashion events, beginning with the HRH Princess Mary's Ball in Aid of the Hospitals of London Combined Appeal on 28 June 1922, which included a fashion parade. A report in *The Sphere* read:

> In the drawing above some of the members of Lady Newnes's 1842 group are seen in the centre of the floor. Although the procession was intended primarily as a review of a century of fashion, Lady Newnes's group wore replicas of the costumes worn by their forebears at the famous Queen Victoria Ball of 1842, so that the costumes of this group went back beyond the prescribed period.

The first dedicated fashion event was the International Beauty Ball and Fashion Parade on 22 October 1926. Twenty years later, in 1946, A Ball and Midnight Parade of Fashion was held – *The Times* reported patriotically on the occasion: 'At midnight last night the floor of the Albert Hall was cleared of dancers and the biggest parade of fashion ever staged in this country began. One hundred and fifty mannequins from twenty-two fashion houses filed slowly under gigantic arc lamps at the rate of six a minute on to the centre of the floor. Each girl was wearing the very latest gowns from British designers. It was the largest show of its kind and demonstrated beyond any doubt the superiority of British design and material.'

8 PROTESTS & POLITICS

Some of the greatest orators of the last 150 years, including Winston Churchill, Marcus Garvey and Emmeline Pankhurst, have used the Hall to deliver their speeches. But the use of the venue for political events has caused some controversy.

93. TEMPLE OF LIBERTY

During the height of the Votes for Women movement, between 1908 and 1913, meetings for either the suffragists, with their peaceful, constitutional approach, or the more militant suffragettes, were held on over twenty occasions. But the Hall, dubbed a 'temple of liberty' by Emmeline Pankhurst, was also the scene of a huge anti-suffrage rally in 1912.

The Women's Social and Political Union, formed in 1903, first met at the Hall in March 1908, with thousands in attendance. An empty chair had been placed on the stage to represent leader Emmeline Pankhurst, thought to be still incarcerated in Holloway Prison. Having been released that very morning, she walked out on stage to rapturous applause. She later recalled: 'A great cry went up from the women as they sprang from their seats and stretched their hands towards me. It was some time before I could see them for my tears, or speak to them for the emotion that shook me like a storm.'

That same year, an infamous incident occurred when suffragette Helen Ogston used a dog whip against men who were trying to eject her from the second tier balcony. The meeting on 5 December, organised by the Women's Liberal Federation, included an address from Chancellor of the Exchequer David Lloyd George, who assured the 8,000 people present that votes for women would be included in the forthcoming Franchise Bill. The speech was interrupted by members of the audience chanting, 'We want deeds, not words.' Tussles broke out as the women, some of whom were chained to their seats, were ejected. Sylvia Pankhurst was expecting violence, and had even pre-arranged a press conference

OPPOSITE: Suffragette with a dog whip at a Women's Liberal Federation (WLF) Meeting, held at the Royal Albert Hall, 5 December 1908.

so that any injuries could be displayed. Even so, she had earlier tried to dissuade Ogston, who claimed she suffered cigar burns and a blow to the chest during her eviction, from taking the dog whip into the Hall.

In the days that followed, a row broke out in the press about whether it was the Liberal Party stewards – who had been told not to use violence – or other men who were responsible for the heavy-handed treatment of the women. In a letter to *The Times*, Ogston stated that she was 'set upon by the stewards and knocked backwards by a man who was sitting in the next box'. She said she used her whip to prevent a 'mauling'. The manager of the Hall denied that the stewards had been violent, and some women present claimed that they had behaved with the 'utmost courtesy'. However, another attendee, Carl Hentschel, wrote to the paper saying: 'To witness a few burly men hurl themselves on some slight and delicate woman, smother her mouth with their coarse hands, carry her bodily and with violence out of the Hall, within a few feet of a cabinet minister, who views the scene with equanimity, was regrettable and scandalous.'

Over the next five years, with a growing number of women being arrested for criminal damage and assault, the Hall's Council became increasingly worried about the militant elements of the movement. Minutes from a meeting in March 1912 show that the Council agreed to let the Women's Social and Political Union hold a meeting that month, on the condition they took out a £10,000 indemnity against any damage.

That same year saw the first rally against votes for women, organised by the National League for Opposing Women's Suffrage. Speaker Lord Curzon explained why women should never have the vote, claiming that were was 'no class in the nation that would not suffer' if women gained the vote, and adding that the move would result in women being thrust into 'operations and activities for which they had neither the aptitude, the training, nor the inclination, which would draw them away from the highest and most responsible functions of womanhood'.

As well as attending their own meetings, the suffragettes went to great lengths to disrupt those of their opponents. In order to gain entry to one meeting, Laura Ainsworth hid under the platform at the end of a concert the night before and was only discovered at ten o'clock the next morning. Another supporter, according to legend, hid in one of the organ pipes with a microphone and was discovered by the caretaker going about his nightly rounds with his dog.

In 1913, the Hall refused a booking request from the Union because of the fear of physical damage to the building, effectively making them the first political party to be banned from the premises. In the run up to the Union's final meeting in April

RIGHT: Handbill for the WSPU (Suffragette) Women's Demonstration to Welcome Mrs Pankhurst on Her Return From America in the Royal Albert Hall, 9 December 1909.

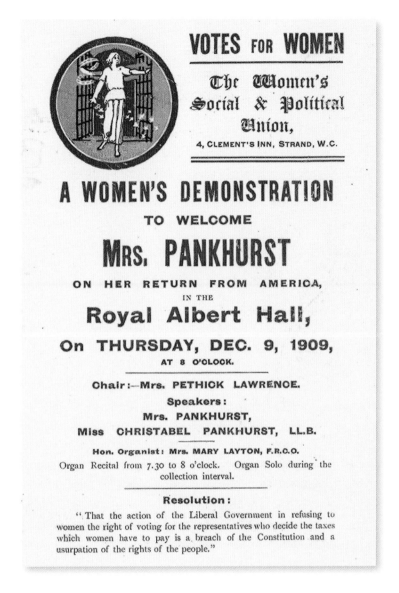

VOTES FOR WOMEN

The Women's Social & Political Union,

4, CLEMENT'S INN, STRAND, W.C.

A WOMEN'S DEMONSTRATION

TO WELCOME

MRS. PANKHURST

ON HER RETURN FROM AMERICA,

IN THE

Royal Albert Hall,

On THURSDAY, DEC. 9, 1909,

AT 8 O'CLOCK.

Chair:—Mrs. PETHICK LAWRENCE.

Speakers:

Mrs. PANKHURST,

Miss CHRISTABEL PANKHURST, LL.B.

Hon. Organist: Mrs. MARY LAYTON, F.R.C.O.

Organ Recital from 7.30 to 8 o'clock. Organ Solo during the collection interval.

Resolution:

"That the action of the Liberal Government in refusing to women the right of voting for the representatives who decide the taxes which women have to pay is a breach of the Constitution and a usurpation of the rights of the people."

that year, Pankhust wrote in *The Suffragette*, 'The Albert Hall meetings have been the landmarks that have shown the public the strength of our movement.'

94. THE GREAT STATESMAN

Winston Churchill, perhaps the most notable prime minister in British history, made twenty-eight speeches at the Hall between 1925 and 1959, many of them at the annual gathering of the Primrose League, a Conservative club set up by his father Lord Randolph Churchill.

During the Second World War on 28 September 1943, Churchill gave a speech at the Hall entitled 'Women's Part in the Struggle' to an exclusively female audience drawn from those in military services, industry and voluntary services. He applauded women's contribution to the war effort and declared there should be 'no fear of the future':

This war effort could not have been achieved had women not marched forward in millions to undertake all kinds of work. Nothing has been grudged, and the bounds of the women's activities have been definitely, vastly and permanently enlarged. It may seem strange that the great advance in the position of women in the world – in industry, in controls of all kinds – should be made in time of war and not in time of peace. One would have thought that in days of peace the progress of women to an ever-larger share in life, work and guidance to the community would have grown, that under violence and fear it would have been cast back. The reverse is true. War is the teacher – a stern, hard, efficient teacher. War has taught us to make vast strides forward toward a far more complete equalisation of the parts to be played by women in society.

As he left the stage, he raised his hand in the familiar 'V for Victory' sign, and thousands of women rose to their feet and returned the gesture. A year later, on America's Thanksgiving Day, he used the Hall to deliver a speech lauding the close ties between the United Kingdon and the United States, saluting America for joining the struggle against the German forces. Standing under a huge picture of Abraham Lincoln, he said: 'We are joined together, shedding our blood side by side, struggling for the same ideals, and joined together until the triumph of the great causes which we serve has been made manifest.'

Churchill's eightieth birthday was celebrated with an impressive concert at the Hall in November 1954 and, in September 2018, his was one of the first Royal Albert Hall Stars – each individually engraved in stone and topped off with a brass star – to be installed under the Hall's canopy.

95. A Powerful Message

On 6 June 1928, the activist Marcus Garvey took to the stage to rail against the 'recurrence' of slavery. The Jamaican-born writer and founder of the Universal Negro Improvement Association already had links with the UK, having worked as a journalist in London before the First World War. Described by *Negro World* as 'the best loved and best hated Negro in the world', he was a controversial figure whose fight for justice for all people of African descent garnered him millions of followers, but whose collaboration with the detested Ku Klux Klan, who shared his wish for racial segregation, also made him many enemies.

Ahead of the Royal Albert Hall speech, *Negro World* commented on the importance of Garvey's visit, saying that it 'cannot be overestimated … The Universal Negro Improvement Association has many powerful friends throughout Europe who see in the program of Marcus Garvey the only guarantee of future world happiness.' He would, the papear said, 'speak to the English

people, as only he can speak, in [sic] behalf of four million Negroes, and the world will be listening.'

On the night, Garvey was joined by celebrated Caribbean soprano Ethel Oughton Clarke and a choir singing spirituals. In his powerful speech, he praised Abraham Lincoln and Queen Victoria 'the Good' for ending the 'rigours of slavery' under which 'we were brutalised; we were maimed; we were killed; we were ravaged in every way', adding:

Do you not know that we have gladly borne your burdens for hundreds of years? The cotton mills of Lancashire, the great shipping port of Liverpool, tell the tale of what we have done as black men for the British Empire. The cotton that you consume … is the product of negro labour. Upon that cotton

PROGRAMME

ROYAL
ALBERT
HALL

OCTOBER
THIRD...
1933

your industry has prospered and you have been able to build the great British Empire of today. Have you no gratitude for a people who have helped with all God gives them? We are not before you tonight asking you to pay us for three hundred years of labour in slavery. No! We are only asking you now for common justice.

Although Garvey was unsuccessful in realising his ambitions for Africa at the time, he was integral in laying the foundations for decolonisation movements in the post-war world. He died from a stroke in London in 1940 at the age of fifty-two, but his ideology went on to influence other movements, including the Rastafari and Black Power movements.

96. EINSTEIN'S THEORY

Ten months after Adolf Hitler came to power in Germany in January 1933, Albert Einstein took to the podium in front of a packed auditorium to deliver a passionate speech against the Nazi suppression of 'intellectual and individual freedom'. Although it was six years before the Second World War broke out, Einstein predicted the looming crisis, asking, 'How can we save mankind and its spiritual acquisitions of which we are the heirs and how can one save Europe from a new disaster?'

The Jewish-German physicist had recently fled Germany with the help of a British organisation called the Academic Assistance Council, created by William Beveridge. In Einstein's homeland, Jewish academics were already losing their jobs, and violence against Jews was escalating, with many having their homes and property confiscated. Einstein warned that, to stem the rise of Fascism, 'We need to keep clearly before us what is at stake, and what we owe to that freedom which our ancestors have won for us after hard struggles.' He then added:

Without such freedom there would have been no Shakespeare, no Goethe, no Newton, no Faraday, no Pasteur and no Lister. There would be no comfortable houses for the mass of people, no railway, no wireless, no protection against epidemics, no cheap books, no culture and no enjoyment of art at all. There would be no machines to relieve the people from the arduous labour needed for the production of the essential necessities of life. Most people would lead a dull life of slavery just as under the ancient despotisms of Asia. It is only men who are free, who create the inventions and intellectual works which to us moderns make life worthwhile.

OPPOSITE: Programme
for the Spain and Culture
event, in aid of Basque
Refugee Children,
featuring artwork by
Picasso, 24 June 1937.

Before the event, which raised £400,000 for the Refugee Assistance
Committee, the *Daily Mail* urged readers to stay away as its proprietor Lord
Rothermere was a supporter of both Adolf Hitler and the British Union of
Fascists, and regarded Einstein as a Communist agitator. However, *The Times*
reported that the scientist was wildly cheered on rising and during his speech,
which was delivered in English and with two Nobel Prize winners, the physicist
Lord Ernest Rutherford and the statesman Austen Chamberlain, in attendance.
Four days after the speech, Einstein sailed to the US for a new life, taking a
position at the Institute of Advanced Study in Princeton. He never returned to
his homeland.

97. BLACKSHIRTS

Hitler's rise to power fuelled growing support for the British Union of Fascists,
formed in 1932 by Oswald Mosley and supported by *Daily Mail* proprietor
Lord Rothermere. The right-wing group booked the Hall for two rallies in 1934,
in April and October. Despite fears of a clash with anti-Fascists, the political
journalist A.J. Cummings commented that the spring meeting, at which Mosley
spoke for ninety minutes without notes, was 'as much like the beginnings of
a political and economic revolution as a sports festival at Wembley'. Mosley
addressed the Hall once again in 1935 but, this time, only ticket-holders were
allowed to enter and a noisy, angry crowd gathered outside and had to be kept in
check by police.

The 'Blackshirts' became increasingly unpopular as the 1930s wore on,
and feelings were running high as they assembled for their next meeting at
the Hall in March 1936 wearing paramilitary uniforms and giving salutes.
A force of 2,500 police was deployed, and only ticket-holders were allowed
within half a mile of the Hall. Despite the best efforts of the authorities,
anti-Fascist protestors infiltrated the event and fights broke out inside –
Mosley was an hour late starting his speech. The event finally convinced
the Council that such extreme political views – and all future rallies by the
Union and the Communist Party – should be banned. These restrictions
led the Labour MP Ellen Wilkinson to raise a question in the House of
Commons, calling for the Hall to be nationalised, and saying that the owner's
ban on 'political meetings except those that support the Government'
amounted to discrimination. Today, each application is judged on its own
merit, the main consideration being the upkeep of law and order and the best
interests of the Hall itself.

Protests & Politics

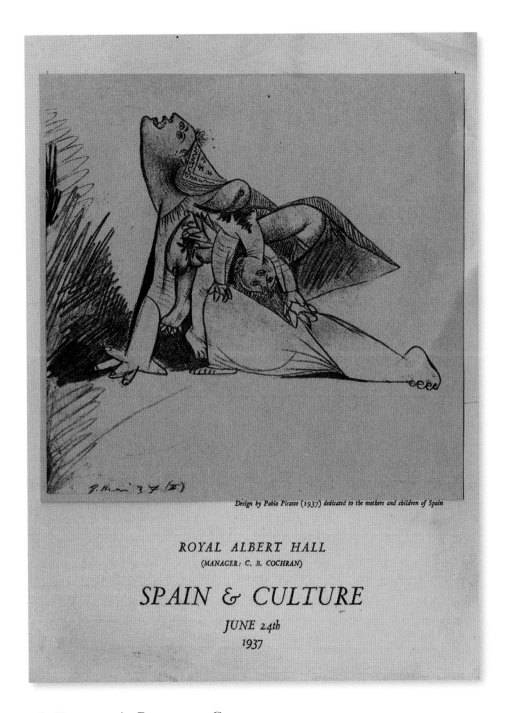

Design by Pablo Picasso (1937) dedicated to the mothers and children of Spain

ROYAL ALBERT HALL

(MANAGER: C. B. COCHRAN)

SPAIN & CULTURE

JUNE 24th
1937

98. ROBESON'S RALLYING CRY

The rising tensions in Europe were further increased by the Spanish Civil War between 1936 and 1939, which saw left-leaning Republicans and their allies battling Franco's Fascist forces. In 1937, American singer and activist Paul Robeson was in the Soviet Union when he was asked to contribute to an anti-Fascist rally on 24 June at the Royal Albert Hall to raise funds to rescue children from the war in Spain. The initial plan was for Robeson to record a speech that would be broadcast to London via radio, but the German authorities threatened to jam the transmission, while the Hall's management had their own reservations about communications originating from a Communist country. Robeson, infuriated, made the recording anyway, later saying, 'Nothing was going to stop me from sending or giving my message to the British public on the subject of Spain.'

On the evening of the rally, Robeson surprised the audience by appearing in person, having flown in specially. Pablo Picasso, who was originally billed to appear and designed the programme's cover, had to pull out, but Robeson stood alongside the likes of the German novelist Heinrich Mann and the Scottish politician Katharine Stewart-Murray, Duchess of Atholl, and stole the show – one audience member, the artist William Townsend, recalled that he 'was the great man of the evening ... his personality eclipsed all others as his speech overwhelmed theirs.'

'Fascism fights to destroy the culture which society has created; created through pain and suffering, through desperate toil, but with unconquerable will and lofty vision,' Robeson told the crowds. The words had added power coming as they did from the son of a slave, whose people had known suffering and oppression at the hands of white Europeans. 'Every artist, every scientist, every writer must decide now where he stands,' he added. 'He has no alternative. There is no standing above the conflict on Olympian heights. There are no impartial observers ... The battlefront is everywhere.' The speech received a lengthy standing ovation.

Robeson returned to the Hall later that year on 19 December for a three-hour rally, where he joined Clement Attlee, Ellen Wilkinson, Herbert Morrison and other Labour Party politicians to attack the Government's support for the international Non-Intervention Agreement over Spain. More than 12,000 people turned up, with the overflow congregating in Hammersmith Town Hall. After passionate speeches from Attlee and Wilkinson, Robeson treated the audience to a rewritten version of 'Ol' Man River' that transformed it from a 'white-person's spiritual' to an unapologetic protest. His performance was the event's finale, and brought the house down.

Robeson had appeared at the Hall long before at the regular Sunday afternoon concerts. With accessible ticket prices that started at three shillings (around £8.60 today), these were hugely popular with music lovers, offering a variety of acts for all musical tastes. On 28 April 1929, Robeson became one of the first black singers to headline at the venue, fresh from his success in the West End production of the hit musical *Show Boat*. In an anthology of writings by and about the American star, *Paul Robeson: The Great Forerunner*, his biographer Marie Seton recalled how he kept the audience enthralled with his sonorous spiritual songs: 'Some tones were so deep they suggested the

Protests & Politics

elemental sound of thunder; others were strangely clear, high sweet and gentle.'
About one spiritual, 'Sometimes I Feel Like a Motherless Child', she wrote:
'There was something almost painful about this massive man with strong,
forceful features speaking in song with such infinitely tender and sorrowful
yearning.' After the success of this concert, Paul settled in London for several
years, and embarked on a UK tour, saying that he found Britain a more tolerant
place than his homeland.

99. Peace in our Time
The historic 'Peace Ballot' organised by the League of Nations Union in 1934
asked the British public five questions in order to ascertain the country's attitude
towards both the League of Nations and collective security. It posed such
questions as 'Should Great Britain remain a Member of the League of Nations?'

and 'Do you consider that, if a nation insists on attacking another, the other nations should combine to compel it to stop?'

The ballot was arranged by the president of the League of Nations Union, Lord Robert Cecil, and, with the horrors of the First World War still vivid in the public mind, his call for disarmament met with huge support. Almost twelve million British adults voted, with the great majority supporting peace and disarmament. The poll was completed in June 1935 and the final results were announced by Cecil at a packed Royal Albert Hall on 27 June. In his speech, he said that Britons have shown 'overwhelming approval' of the collective system: 'The people ... know well enough what peace means, and they care for it with every fibre of their being. Do not think that the ballot is an end in itself. It is just a stage in the struggle for peace. It must be made the starting point for further exertion.' Two years after this meeting, Cecil won the Nobel Peace Prize.

100. MISS WORLD AND THE ANGRY BRIGADE

Although the Miss World beauty pageant was held at the Hall on twenty occasions between 1969 and 1988, there is one particular year that stands out as

the most memorable. In 1970, amidst a growing feminist backlash against the
contest, around fifty protestors from the Women's Liberation Movement let off
stink and smoke bombs and bombarded host Bob Hope with flour bombs and
rotten vegetables. Chants of 'We're not beautiful, we're not ugly, we're angry'
were broadcast on the BBC's live feed. Hope, who was prevented from leaving
the stage when he tried to flee, countered with the unfortunate statement:
'Anybody who wants to interrupt something as beautiful as this must be on
some kind of dope.'

However, the protests went much further than many realised. The evening
before, a small home-made bomb had been placed in one of the BBC's

outside-broadcast trucks in an attempt to disrupt the live feed beaming
the Miss World pageant to twenty-three million viewers. While the bomb
did explode, the damage was minimal and the broadcast went ahead – this
more serious attack was the work of an anarchist group, the Angry Brigade,
believed to be responsible for around twenty-five bombings between 1970
and 1972.

Protestor Linda Clarke remembers: 'We were told we were going to be given
a signal. We all had to dress up pretty fine and I remember having this big bag
because it had this football-clapper thing and flour bombs. We were planted all
over the Albert Hall. We were all very pleased that whoever did the signal, it
was when Bob Hope was standing there. We didn't want to attack the women
themselves at all.'

Remarkably, after police ejected the demonstrators, the show went ahead and
twenty-two-year-old Miss Grenada, Jennifer Hosten, was crowned Miss World.
She was awarded a £900 tiara and £4,600 in cash, the latter amounting to around
£70,000 today. 'I do not really know enough about what they were demonstrating
against,' she declared. 'All I know is that it has been a wonderful experience
competing for the Miss World title.' Oddly, one of the judges of the pageant was
Grenada's premier, Eric Gairy.

While the Miss World pageant continued that night, and still takes place
today, the feminist movement had made its voice heard – growing opposition
to the event led to the BBC dropping the broadcast in 1988, which was also the
last year it was held at the Hall. Fifty years on, the events that night inspired
the film *Misbehaviour*, starring Keira Knightley, Keeley Hawes and Gugu
Mbatha-Raw.

101. NELSON MANDELA

During a four-day visit to the UK in 1996 as a guest of the Queen, Nelson
Mandela decided to repay her hospitality with an evening of music at the Hall
on 11 July entitled Two Nations Celebrate. The South African President went
on a walkabout, meeting and greeting the Hall staff with his daughter Zenani
Mandela-Dlamini, the Queen, the Duke of Edinburgh and the Prince of Wales,
before watching the concert from the Queen's Box.

Mandela's chosen hosts were the poets Benjamin Zephaniah and Mzwakhe
Mbuli, and the cultural collaboration saw South African artists Bayete,
Ladysmith Black Mambazo and Hugh Masekela take to the stage along with Phil
Collins, Quincy Jones and Tony Bennett. Up in the usually sedate Queen's Box,

Zenani began dancing, and soon her father and the Prince of Wales were swaying too. *The Daily Telegraph* reported that they were joined by the Queen, 'who has seldom been known to boogie in public'.

Former head steward Linda Clifford was responsible for showing the Queen and Nelson Mandela to their box. 'The Queen came to the Hall with Nelson Mandela,' she recalls. 'I was in charge of the door eight lift by myself. The lift used to play up, the doors would close and then re-open. And it did it then. Eventually we got there. The Duke of Edinburgh walked past me and said, "You'll get a medal for that later."

9 HAVING A BALL

Although balls are rare events at the Hall today, the venue has seen some extremely lavish, colourful and riotous dances over the years. With guests ranging from royalty to scullery maids, many happy party-goers and artists have danced the night away within the Hall's walls.

102. A Savage Start

The first ball at the Hall was thrown by the Savage Club, an exclusive London gentlemen's club set up in 1857 for men 'connected with literature and the fine arts'. The Savage Club Entertainment & Costume Ball, held on 11 July 1883, was attended by the Prince and Princess of Wales, and began with a sumptuous champagne dinner followed by entertainments, including a midnight performance of a 'buffalo dance' by club members dressed in Native American costumes. Tickets were on sale to the public, although each application was scrutinised by a club committee and accepted or declined as it saw fit. Cheap tickets costing five shillings got the buyer only as far as the gallery, where they were merely permitted to watch the festivities below, but not to join in.

Most attendees went to great lengths to find fancy-dress apparel, and the press reported that London shops had been 'raided for costumes' and theatre props had been borrowed by those with West End connections. Although such costumes were not compulsory, those who didn't deck themselves out were banned from the dance floor so that the view of the 'various and variegated costumes should not be spoilt with the intermixture of plain black and white'. Even at three o'clock in the morning, when two gentlemen attempted to wend their way onto the floor, the stewards politely 'requested they withdraw'.

Although reviews of the event were not entirely favourable, the Hall itself came in for high praise. The press reported: 'The Albert Hall – for capacity, grandeur of line, and beauty of proportion – is unrivalled in the world for the

RIGHT: Illustration of
The Chelsea Arts Club
Annual Ball – 'Venetian
Carnival', 6 March
1912.

OPPOSITE: Programme
for The Chelsea Arts Club
Annual Ball, 31 December
1951.

purposes of a fancy ball … The costumes were probably the most varied ever
seen together, and many were remarkably artistic, accurate, and splendid.'

103. THE ELEPHANT (NOT) IN THE ROOM

The Chelsea Arts Club's Ball was a riotous costume party first held on New
Year's Eve 1919, and then every year between 1928 and 1958. The exclusive
Chelsea Arts Club was set up in 1891 by a group of artists, including James
McNeill Whistler, and its balls grew increasingly imaginative and extravagant
as time went on, with such themes as 'Dazzle', 'Prehistoric' and 'Old English'.
In 1929, the organisers proposed bringing an elephant into the arena as the
centrepiece for the ball, but the move was vetoed by the Hall's Council on the
grounds that the Great Floor, which needed to be in place to accommodate the
large number of diners and dancers, would not take the weight of this exotic
guest. This led to a ban on live animals at the Hall, which stands today.

Guests at the Chelsea Arts Club Balls enjoyed dinner and a mini-carnival first.
Then, at the stroke of midnight, the event descended into an orgy of destruction,
as floats and papier-mâché models, designed and built by art students each year,
were ceremonially smashed to pieces at midnight. Afterwards, there was dancing
and drinking until five o'clock in the morning, when breakfast was served.
Extravagant costumes were encouraged and, at one ball in the 1930s, a whole host
of students from St Martin's School of Art painted themselves gold and stood
on the floats, only to all come crashing down during the midnight destruction. In
1953, guests paraded through the streets wearing their papier-mâché heads before
entering the Hall.

As the biggest costume party in the capital, the Chelsea Arts Club Ball gained
international notoriety, with America's *LIFE* magazine observing that 'scanty
dress was more the rule than the exception'. The event also appeared in David

Having a Ball

BELOW: Guests in fancy
dress at The Chelsea Arts
Club Annual Ball,
31 December 1951.

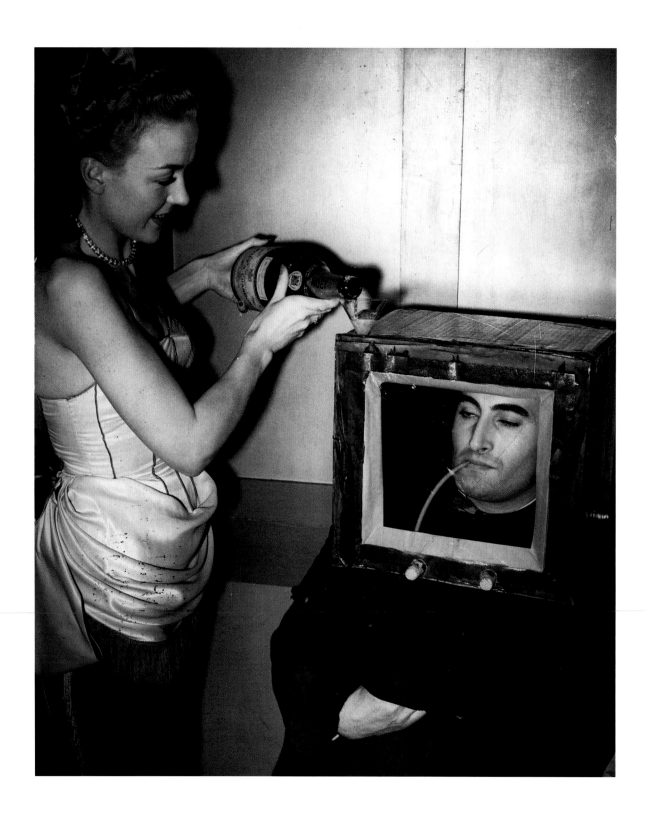

Having a Ball

RIGHT: Chelsea Arts Club
Ball, held at the Royal
Albert Hall in 1952.

RIGHT: Students in fancy
dress outside The Chelsea
Arts Club Annual Ball,
31 December 1953.

Having a Ball

Lord Sackville as Thomas Sackville Earl of Dorset.

Lean's 1949 film *The Passionate Friends*, while Paul Thomas Anderson's 2017 film *Phantom Thread* included an exquisite recreation of the ball's 1950s heyday. The party came to an end in the early hours of 1959, when a smoke bomb was let off in the Hall, which sent choking revellers running for the exit, and leaving some in pain. The Council declined the application for the event the following year. The Chelsea Arts Club Ball did return to the Hall three more times – in 1984, 1985 and 1992 – but without the elaborate costumes and floats.

Peter Blake has recalled a Chelsea Arts Club Ball he attended in the 1950s, along with the painter Dick Smith:

We were carrying the central float and guarding it as well. The object of the crowd was to destroy the float, so you had guards guarding the floats and official guards guarding everything. The guards mistook me for an attacker and they must have thrown me to the ground. I woke up in the early hours of the morning in a dusty corner of the Albert Hall, having been very drunk and knocked unconscious. So that was my last memory of the Chelsea Arts Club Ball, which is probably appropriate!

104. Midsummer Night's Dream

While the Chelsea Arts Club Ball was riotous, the most lavish of events was the Shakespeare Memorial Ball, held on 20 June 1911. Renowned architect Edwin Landseer Lutyens transformed the Hall into a Tudor garden in an Italianate style. Yew trees clipped into shapes decorated the edges of the Great Floor, with vines hanging from the bowers weighed down with grapes, positioned just high enough to prevent the revellers helping themselves. The circle was transformed into a sloping green lawn and the gallery pillars were hidden by groves of cypress trees, with blue fabric stretched from the sides of the ceiling to its middle, creating the blue sky of a glorious summer day.

Among the 3,000 people who attended were Prime Minister Herbert Asquith and Winston and Clementine Churchill. As the event was scheduled just two days before the coronation of George V, it was attended by more members of European royalty than any event in the Hall's history. The dinner and dancing were followed by tableaux depicting scenes from Shakespeare's plays, with the guests dressed as dukes, cardinals and courtiers from the Elizabethan period. Many of those taking part were descendants of the very aristocrats they were playing, including the Howards, Talbots, Cecils, Burghleys, Fortescues, Lytteltons, Hamiltons and Comptons.

LADY MALCOLM'S SERVANTS' BALL
(TENTH ANNIVERSARY)

ROYAL ALBERT HALL,
Tuesday, Nov. 14th, 1933
9 p.m.——to——3 a.m.

*In aid of the West End
Hospital for Nervous
Diseases.*

The event, which raised £10,000 for the Shakespeare Memorial Fund, was praised in an article in the *Dominion* magazine that read: 'Those who were fortunate enough to see it have something to recollect all their lives. For splendour, for beauty, for perfection of harmonious colouring, for brilliance of general effect, nothing to compare with it has been seen in our time.'

105. SERVANTS' NIGHT OUT

It wasn't just the upper classes who got to enjoy costume balls at the Albert Hall. Once a year, between 1930 and 1938, domestic servants swapped their black uniforms and white aprons for fancy dress, to enjoy Lady Malcolm's Servants' Balls. It was a rare chance for those who lived life below stairs to socialise with other servants and dance until midnight in a grand setting, at a price affordable

Having a Ball

for even the lowest paid. In 1986, the *Daily Mirror* received a letter from a reader who had been servant in a house in Grosvenor Square, and recalled going to the ball as a thirteen-year-old, describing it as a 'thrilling, glamorous' evening for servants for whom a night out was a rare event, and whose wages were usually sent home to support their family.

The event's founder was the social reformer Lady Jeanne Malcolm, the wife of the Labour MP Ian Malcolm. She was the only daughter of infamous beauty Lillie Langtry, who counted the Prince of Wales (later to become Edward VII) among her lovers. She held the first Servants' Ball in a small venue in Kensington with 360 guests, but the event grew every year and eventually moved to the Royal Albert Hall. Lady Malcolm stipulated fancy dress so that those who could not afford expensive evening dress need not be embarrassed, and prizes for the best costumes were awarded by well-known figures from the music world. She also caused something of a sensation at one ball, in 1929, when an American newspaper reported that she danced with her butler, leaving London society wondering how she could now retain a dignified position around her staff.

The cheap tickets and fancy-dress element attracted many members of the underground gay scene in London. As homosexuality was illegal, the organisers considered them 'undesired elements', and in 1935 a warning was added to the event's ticket declaring that: 'No Man Impersonating a Woman will be admitted.' Lady Malcolm also became increasingly frustrated with the number of non-servants attending and, in November 1936, wrote a letter to *The Times* stating:

> Each year I notice at the ball a growing number of people, who to be frank, are not of the class for whom the ball is designed. It is, what it calls itself, a Servants' Ball, and I am jealous that it shall go on deserving that name. It is because I have the double aim of helping a hospital and of giving London's domestic servants the real chance of a big night out that I keep the tickets so low.

The high profile of the Servants' Balls also had another unfortunate side effect. When the Malcolms' London home was raided by burglars on the night of the 1930 ball, police assumed that the perpetrators knew that Lady Malcolm, her husband and all the servants would be at the Royal Albert Hall. The risk of such burglaries was thought by many to be the reason the Servants' Balls ceased after 1938, but the onset of the Second World War is a much more likely explanation. Lady Malcolm went on to head the Marylebone Housing Association for many years and was awarded an MBE for her Red Cross work. She died in 1964.

Shopworkers at London's department stores were also rewarded for hard work with an annual ball, with Selfridges, Whiteleys and Barkers all holding their own events at the Hall. From the 1950s, John Lewis, Marks & Spencer and Freemans also threw annual balls at the venue.

106. A Roaring Success

The 'Roaring Twenties' was the era of the flapper and dances crazes such as the Black Bottom and the Charleston. On 15 December 1926, a spectacular

OPPOSITE LEFT:
Programme for Lady Malcolm's Servants' Ball's Tenth Anniversary Event, 14 November 1933.

OPPOSITE RIGHT:
Programme for Guild of British Creative Designers Fashion Ball, 1 October 1947.

RIGHT: Programme
from the Charleston Ball
and Competition, 15
December 1926.

Having a Ball

dance competition – the Charleston Ball – was held at the Hall, with prizes that included a trip to Paris on Imperial Airways, a case of whisky, and official Colman's Mustard Club pots. Fred Astaire was one of the judges and the brilliant American performer Florence Mills was among the dancers. Among the entrants to the competition's troupe category were 'The Princess Charming Girls', 'The Lido Lady Girls' and 'The Sunny Tiller Girls'. Future impresario Lew Grade, then a clothing salesman, was crowned the World Charleston Champion and the title propelled him into show business, changing the whole course of his life.

For the ball, the auditorium was decorated with thousands of coloured balloons and special lights. Music was provided by the Charleston Band, Jack Hylton's Kit Cat Band and Johnny Hudgins' Plantation Orchestra, performing in rotation throughout the night. The event lasted until five o'clock in the morning, with its promoter Charles Cochran later recalled the finale:

> It was the unexpected and final entrance from the organ, down the steps, into the arena of Florence Mills, Johnny Hudgins, and the Blackbirds which sent the house wild with enthusiasm. Johnny Hudgins was encored and encored until it seemed as if his marvellously unattached limbs would fall off. One would have thought nobody could follow him. But the thunder increased as the slim body of Florence Mills went through more amusing contortions than you could imagine in a nightmare.

107. THE SWINGING SIXTIES

The 1960s saw hems rising ever higher, and in 1967 the Hall played host to the *Daily Mirror*'s Gorgeous Girls Gala: The World's First Mini-Skirt Ball. Perhaps not something for the modern age, the event was a hit at the time. Bandleaders including Acker Bilk and Georgie Fame took to the stage. and there were performances by Lulu, the Bachelors and the Go-Go's. There were famous faces in the arena too, with Tom Jones, DJ Simon Dee and iconic designer Mary Quant among the guests. The event marked one hundred days since the *Mirror* had launched its 'Gorgeous Girls Gallery', and the one hundred women granted this dubious accolade so far were the guests of honour.

From the 1970s to the 1990s, the Airlines Balls for employees of major airlines, and the Valentine Balls on 14 February hosted by the likes of Sam Fox and Liz Hurley, both became annual fixtures. The Black & White Balls, which were held from 1994 to 1996, took on more of a club vibe – DJs such as Paul Oakenfold and Brandon Block performed in front of a psychedelic Alice-in-Wonderland themed set, with laser shows and huge sound systems.

RIGHT: Programme for *Daily Mirror's* Gorgeous Girls Gala – The World's First Mini-Skirt Ball, 21 October 1967.

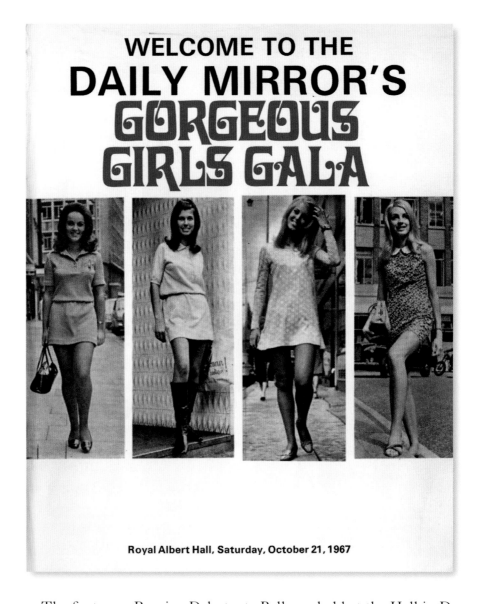

WELCOME TO THE
DAILY MIRROR'S
GORGEOUS GIRLS GALA

Royal Albert Hall, Saturday, October 21, 1967

The first-ever Russian Debutante Ball was held at the Hall in December 2013. Drawing on the British tradition of 'coming-out parties', at which girls from aristocratic backgrounds who have recently reached adulthood are introduced to society, the event is open to young men and women from across the globe. The evening opens with hundreds of debutantes, all dressed in white floor-length gowns, long white gloves and tiaras, taking to the dance floor with their tuxedoed escorts to the 'Waltz of the Flowers' from Tchaikovsky's *The Nutcracker*. The 'debs' at the ball need not necessarily hail from nobility, but they do need to know the Viennese waltz and a smattering of other ballroom dances.

The annual event only came to the Albert Hall for one season, but was deemed to be a triumph. Guests were treated to performances by the Royal Philharmonic Orchestra and the prima ballerina of the Bolshoi Ballet, Evgenia Obraztsova, as well as a collaboration by three of Russia's most celebrated tenors, Dmitry Korchak, Daniil Shtoda and Vladimir Galouzine. *The Spectator* reported that 'Bentleys lined South Kensington' on the night, and that one Russian attendee made a speech alluding to the ongoing tensions between London and Moscow: 'We are not an aggressive people, we love balls. We want to show that to the people of Britain. Rather than anything aggressive that might be happening right now we want to portray an image of security.'

108. IN COMPETITION

Ballroom dancing has had a home at the Hall since 1928, when the Amateur Ballroom Dancing Championship was held in January. Former world champion and renowned band leader Victor Sylvester and his wife Dorothy were among the judges, as was Santos Casani, author of *Casani's Home Teacher: Ballroom Dancing Made Easy*, with twenty-eight couples competing in total. In 1953, the First International Professional and Amateur Ballroom Dancing Championships, presented by promoter Elsa Wells, was held at the Hall. Now known as the International Ballroom Dancing Championships, it remains one of the most glittering social events in the dance calendar. Among the names that have danced over the years are Len Goodman, dancing in his first ever international competition at the age of twenty; Shirley Ballas, who won the professional crown in 1995; and *Strictly Come Dancing* stars Neil and Katya Jones, who won as amateurs in 2011.

Folk dance also has a rich history at the Hall, with the English Folk Dance and Song Society throwing festivals between 1927 and 1984 that featured groups of Morris dancers from around the country. At the 1959 festival, members of the Royal Ballet School performed a fusion of classical ballet and techniques from the traditional English folk dancing – the result was described in *The Times* as possessing 'a lightness and freedom of movement that looked at once natural and skilful'. In 1980, a dance entitled 'The Streets of London' incorporated metal dustbins into the dance as props.

RIGHT: Sixth International Professional and Amateur Ballroom Dancing Championships, 30 October 1958.

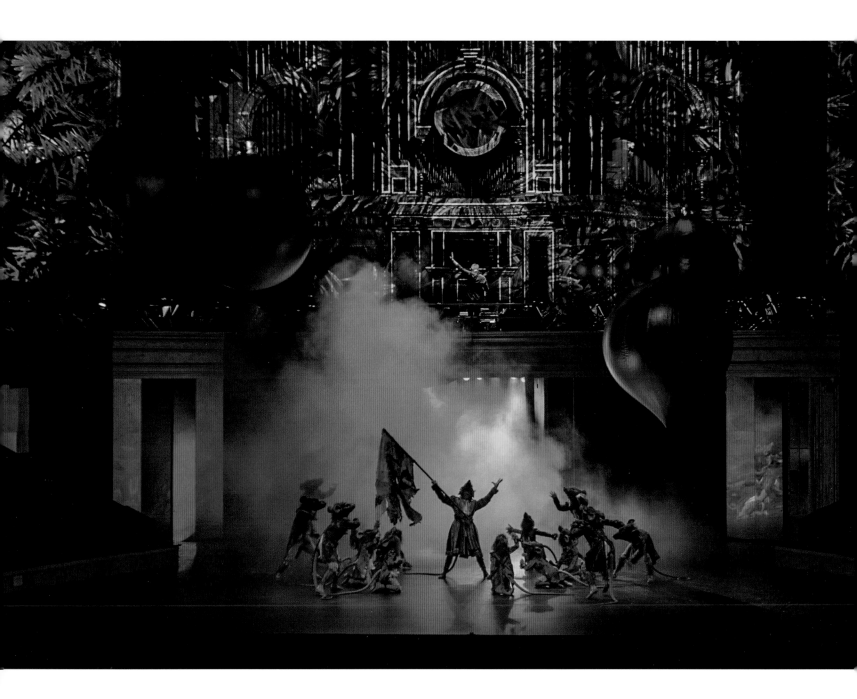

10 OPERA, BALLET & MUSICALS

The Royal Albert Hall's spacious auditorium lends itself to productions with large casts and lavish sets. In 1920 s and 1930s, the cast of a Royal Choral Society production of Samuel Coleridge-Taylor's *The Song of Hiawatha* numbered over 1,000, and tents had to be erected in Kensington Gardens for use as temporary changing rooms. Today, the changing-room space has been extended and operas, musicals and ballets are frequently put on in the Hall.

109. THE OPERA HOUSE

The Hall's association with opera stretches back to the laying of the foundation stone in 1867, when the orchestra and band of the Royal Italian Opera in Covent Garden performed. In July 1871, shortly after the Hall's opening, Her Majesty's Opera Concert was staged. Despite its title, Queen Victoria was not present at the event – it was so called because the choruses and ensemble pieces were performed by the chorus of Her Majesty's Opera House. Since then, the venue has been used as an opera house many times, welcoming such companies as the Kirov Opera and the national operas of Romania, Latvia and Ukraine, as well as productions from Glyndebourne and the Royal Opera House.

One of the most frequent visitors is the Chisinau National Opera from Moldova, which staged ten productions between 1999 and 2005, including Giacomo Puccini's *Turandot* and Giuseppe Verdi's *Aida*. From 1978, promoter Victor Hochhauser brought in talent from around the world, including Russia, for regular Grand Opera Gala nights, with the last one being held in 2010. Star performances included Alfie Boe, Natasha Marsh, Alan Opie, Dimitar Damjanov and Lesley Garrett. Among the other opera giants who have performed in the Hall are Luciano Pavarotti, Joan Sutherland, Renée Fleming, Plácido Domingo,

Opera, Ballet & Musicals

LEFT: The cast of
Verdi's 'Aida', directed by
Stephen Medcalf at the
Royal Albert Hall,
22 February 2012.

BELOW: Tiziana Carraro
(Amneris) during Verdi's
Aida, directed by Stephen
Medcalf at the Royal
Albert Hall, 22 February
2012.

Anna Netrebko, Enrico Caruso, Montserrat Caballé, José Carreras, Cecilia Bartoli, Jussi Björling, Juan Diego Flórez and Kiri Te Kanawa.

In recent years, promoter Raymond Gubbay has been responsible for bringing numerous opera-in-the-round productions to the Hall, including Puccini's *La Bohème* and *Tosca,* Bizet's *Carmen,* Verdi's *Aida* and Puccini's *Madam Butterfly*. He also produces the annual performance of Carl Orff's *Carmina Burana*, which brings four hundred voices together in harmony and has now been seen by 50,000 people.

The world-renowned Glyndebourne Festival Opera has brought many productions to the venue, including the 2013 staging of Benjamin Britain's *Billy Budd*, conducted by Andrew Davies. There was no set, but somehow the arena was successfully transformed into HMS *Indomitable*, the ship on which

RIGHT: Structural engineers Ordish and Grover helped Scott design the 20,000 sq. ft of wrought iron and glass while the metal frame was built by the Fairbairn Engineering Company.

the story takes place, with the balconies used to create a bowl effect and the London Philharmonic Orchestra acting as the hull of the ship, backed by the Glyndebourne Chorus dressed in full naval uniform. The steps at the front of the stage doubled as the below-deck area and the highest balcony became the masts and yardarm of the ship. *The Guardian* reported: 'An unforgettable evening left a buzzing hall of people and a huge crowd cheering by the stage door. Such was the deserved praise for this beautiful performance.'

The Hall has also been instrumental in bringing opera to a whole new generation through its Education & Outreach programme. In November 2019, six hundred musicians from schools across Newham came together to perform in the Newham Community Opera's *Full Circle* production at the Music for Youth Proms.

110. PRIMA BALLERINAS
A stunning fan-shaped programme for the Versailles Ball on 5 June 1913 marks one of only two occasions at which Anna Pavlova danced at the Hall. The prima ballerina was at the height of her fame, having left her native Russia to make London her home the previous year. The ball, which raised money for needy soldiers, was attended by Queen Mary and sixteen royal princes and princesses.

Opera, Ballet & Musicals

BELOW: Dancer rosining
their shoes during 'Swan
Lake' at the Royal Albert
Hall, 14 June 2004.

Opera, Ballet & Musicals

Opera, Ballet & Musicals

OPPOSITE: Princess Diana with the English National Ballet for the Tchaikovsky's 'Swan Lake' Royal Gala Performance, June 1997.

Pavlova danced with fellow Russian Ivan Novikoff, who often partnered her.

Pavlova is among the many ballet stars who have danced at the Hall, including Anton Dolin and Alicia Markova, both of whom performed at Princess Seraphina Astafieva's Anglo-Russian Ballet in 1923. South African ballerina Nadia Nerina appeared with David Blair three times at the Hall between 1958 and 1963, while the Russian prima ballerina Ulyana Lopatkina danced at an evening celebrating her compatriot Igor Zelensky in 2004. The great British star Margot Fonteyn danced the 'Pas de Deux' from Sergei Prokofiev's *Cinderella* with her frequent partner Michael Soames during a televised International Celebrity Festival in 1958. Princess Diana's favourite dancer, Wayne Sleep, appeared at the Hall with Tamara Rojo and Darcey Bussell on 15 September 1998 in Explosive Dance. This special event in aid of the British Red Cross Anti-Personnel Landmines Campaign was dedicated to the Princess, who had died the year before.

Many top ballet companies have appeared at the Hall, including the Bolshoi, the Kirov, the Moscow State, and the Georgian and Ukrainian state dance companies. English National Ballet is closely associated with the Hall, and chose the venue for its fortieth-anniversary celebration gala in 1990. The star-studded evening saw the celebrated French ballerina Sylvie Guillem dance to Maurice Ravel's *Bolero*. In 2017, the Birmingham Royal Ballet brought Tchaikovsky's *The Nutcracker* to the Hall for the first time, and the stunning production has now become an annual event.

III. SWANNING AROUND

English National Ballet's *Swan Lake*, which ran for twelve performances from 29 May 1997, was the first 'ballet in the round' at the Hall. The innovative format, which saw the production take place in the centre of the arena, with the audience on all sides, was created by Derek Deane and showcased the talents of the brilliant Italian dancer Roberto Bolle. The arena was turned into an azure lake for the huge production, and a record-breaking sixty 'swans' in white tutus fanned out across the arena, creating spectacular shapes and formations that could be seen clearly from all sides of the auditorium. The run included a Royal Gala Night, attended by Princess Diana. 'When the swans make their first entrance, wave after wave of them, it's awesome,' read one review of the production in *The Observer*. 'To see them move and breathe as one is profoundly touching.'

Louise Halliday, now the Hall's director of external affairs, was a dancer with English National Ballet. She appeared in the production, and remembers the Gala Night clearly:

> There was a sense of something momentous happening. Ballet in the round was new and different. I remember that night, the response from the audience gave me goose-bumps. There was no barrier between us and the audience. We performed all around the world and the Royal Albert Hall was the best place in the world because the communication between performers and audience is so immediate. You can see the whites of people's eyes when you're on stage and

RIGHT: Vadim
Muntagirov, Daria
Klimentova and dancers
performing Tchaikovsky's
Swan Lake at the Royal
Albert Hall, 11 June
2013.

Opera, Ballet & Musicals

it's a real shared experience. As a performer, rather than being removed from the audience, you are among them, and that's truly special.

Since its premiere, the Tchaikovsky ballet has returned to the Hall annually and has been seen by half a million people. English National Ballet has staged many more ballets in the round at the Hall over the last two decades, including Tchaikovsky's *Sleeping Beauty* and Prokofiev's *Cinderella* and *Romeo and Juliet*, the last of which brought one hundred dancers to the arena.

112. FULL STEAM AHEAD

The first fully staged musical was *Show Boat*, which steamed into the Hall on 10 June 2006. This brand new in-the-round production of the Broadway classic, directed by Francesca Zambello, featured a full-sized Mississippi steamboat in the centre of the arena, surrounded by a 'river' created by set designer Peter J. Davidson.

Originally premiered in New York in 1927, the spectacular musical, set on the theatre boat *Cotton Blossom*, was written by Oscar Hammerstein II and P.G. Wodehouse with music composed by Jerome Kern, and tackle themes of love, loss and racial prejudice. In Zambello's production, the seventy-strong cast, split equally between black and white actors, are seen to overcome a huge divide and, at the finale, every couple dancing is interracial.

'The first musical to be staged at the Albert Hall, *Show Boat* is a logical choice for such a big theatre,' observed *The Independent*. 'It's a great big show, not only for the size of its cast but for its ravishing music, its historic importance, its span of time and space, and its themes.'

113. A SONDHEIM CELEBRATION

To celebrate the eight-fifth birthday of composer Stephen Sondheim, Craig Revel Horwood brought the rarely staged musical *Follies* to the Royal Albert Hall in 2015. The show boasted a spectacular cast that included American actress Christine Baranski, West End star Ruthie Henshall, opera singer Russell Watson, impressionist Alistair McGowan, former *EastEnders* star Anita Dobson, and Betty Buckley, who starred in the original Broadway version of *Cats*.

The show, which centres on the lives of former showgirls languishing in unhappy marriages, has a host of well-known songs, including 'Losing My Mind', 'Broadway Baby' and 'I'm Still Here'. It was only the second time *Follies* had been staged in London, the first being in 1971, and it went on to return in

Opera, Ballet & Musicals

2017, this time directed by Dominic Cooke at the National Theatre. Looking back at the 2015 production, Horwood recalls:

> We were doing one matinee and one evening performance and we only had the morning to get the set ready because it was booked out beforehand. It was tight for time and really fraught. But the Royal Albert Hall is a wonderful venue and I love that you can use the whole space. I performed there as a dancer in 1998, for Andrew Lloyd Webber's fiftieth birthday, and there was raised stage in the centre of the arena, which was brilliant. Standing in the centre of the Hall and looking out to the audience is extraordinary, the most amazing feeling ever.

The Royal Albert Hall frequently celebrates musicals by showcasing works in orchestral concerts, with past productions including *Kristina* and *Chess* by Björn Ulvaeus and Benny Andersson from ABBA, the Musicals Singalong in 1995, and A Celebration of Classic MGM Film Musicals Prom in 2009.

114. A FOND FAREWELL

Cuban ballet star Carlos Acosta chose the Royal Albert Hall to kick off his farewell tour in October 2016, after announcing he would be hanging up his ballet shoes. Recognised as one of the most outstanding dancers of his generation, he had an unparalleled career as a classical ballet dancer before retiring from the Royal Ballet after seventeen years.

For this special performance, Acosta was joined on stage by some of his contemporaries from the Royal Ballet ,including Yuhui Choe, Ryoichi Hirano and Sarah Lamb, as well as Cuban dancers Gabriela Lugo and Luis Valle. He performed extracts from ballet classics including Kenneth MacMillan's *Winter Dreams*, *Mayerling* and *Requiem*, George Balanchine's *Apollo* and Marius Petipa's *Don Quixote*.

'The leaps may be a few inches closer to the ground, the energy slightly more languid but there is no doubt that there will be a great big Carlos Acosta-shaped hole in classical ballet at the end of this tour,' reported *The Stage*. 'Clearly moved by the response, he was in tears at the end. He wasn't the only one.'

The Cuban superstar returned to the Hall to celebrate thirty years in dance with a sell-out run of four nights in October 2018. He was joined by his Havana dance company, Acosta Danza, and the show included stomping extracts from *Carmen*, first directed by Acosta in 2015, and Christopher Bruce's *Rooster*, set to music from the Rolling Stones.

Great Revival Meetings

In the ROYAL ALBERT HALL

LONDON

11 HATCHED, MATCHED & DESPATCHED

The Hall was registered as a place of public worship on 1 December 1891, after a long-running dispute over Sunday concerts. In the 1870s, the Lord's Day Observance Society had been successful in petitioning the Hall to abandon a series of concerts held on Sundays by the secular National Sunday League, yet the Hall eventually overturned this decision and recommenced the concerts in 1877, with free entry for the 'deserving poor'. The dispute continued throughout the 1880s, until the Council decided to obtain a licence making the Hall a place of public worship, which it finally received in 1891. However, there had already been a few religious and spiritual events before this – in 1884 John Hamilton-Gordon, the Earl of Aberdeen, requested to use the Hall for a service to celebrate Dwight Lyman Moody, an American evangelist, who was returning home after a long trip to the UK. Since receiving its licence, the Hall has been the venue for a number of legal and religious ceremonies, including a funeral. It's even hosted one infamous seance.

115. MISSION ACCOMPLISHED

The Hall has played host to many religious figures and organisations throughout the years, including Billy Graham, the Salvation Army and almost one hundred meetings of the Missionary Society, which gathered to bid farewell to members who were about to go abroad to preach the gospel. In 1905, two extraordinary evangelists crossed the Atlantic to bring their own brand of religious fervour

TORREY & ALEXANDER MISSION.

THE GREAT CHILDREN'S MISSION, ROYAL ALBERT HALL.   *Copyright Photo.,* COOK, 319, FULHAM ROAD.

Below: Programme
for Society for the
Propagation of the Gospel
in Foreign Parts' Birthday
Pageant 29–31 April
1927.

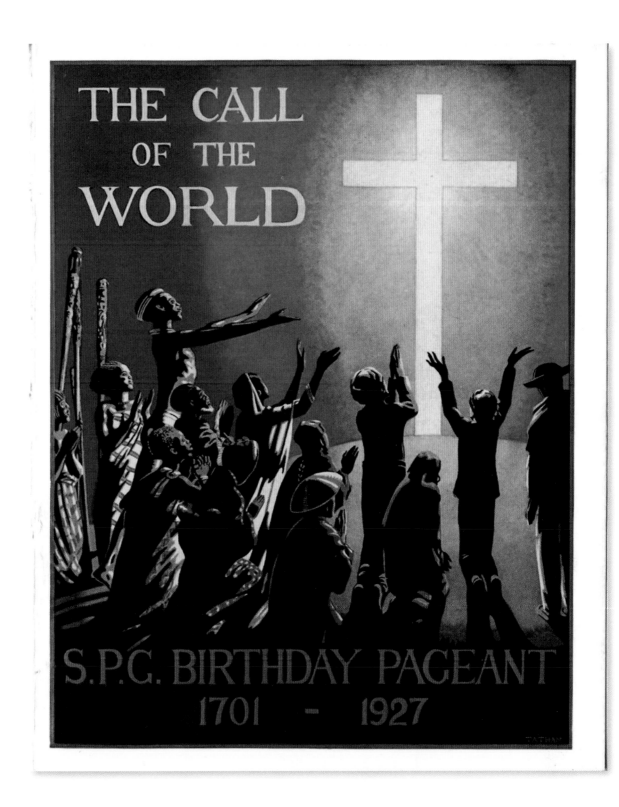

to our shores. Over seven weeks, from 4 February to 19 March, the Torrey-Alexander Mission – led by Americans Charles Alexander and Reuben Torrey – managed to convert 7,000 audience members including Lord Arthur Kinnaird, a leading light in the Church of Scotland, as well as other notables of the era.

Alexander, whose reputation had preceded him, was a lean, clean-shaven preacher with a fervent glint in his eye. His first words, delivered from a red-baize speaker's block on the stage, broke the ice. 'If there is anyone here who has influence with the man who runs the lights, please tell him to turn them up,' he said. 'We can't see the words.' The lights were duly raised and the first hymns began, before Torrey, a dapper middle-aged man with a neatly pointed beard and lustrous moustache, continued the message of joy.

The evening ended with a stirring rendition of the pair's catchy theme tune 'The Glory Song', before those who wished to convert were asked to stand up and confess Christ. Only a handful obliged on the first night, but the following evening netted three hundred converts and the numbers snowballed through the coming weeks. At the end of the mission, 7,000 packed into the Hall for Convert's Night, open only to those who had seen the light, and the divine double act issued a helpful table of their achievements with the following figures:

Sermons preached by Dr Torrey 75
Words uttered 500,000
Hymns sung 400
Letters received by Dr Torrey 5,000
Letters received by Mr Alexander 3,000
Applications for tickets and general letters 1,200,000
Choir 3,000
Workers and helpers 500
Number of visitors 770,000
Converts 7,000

116. Saving Souls

American evangelist Aimee Semple McPherson presided over mass baptisms in the Hall in November 1928, with 1,000 converts taking the plunge in a huge water tank representing the River Jordan. McPherson, a faith healer and founder of the Foursquare Church, was a colourful character who famously disappeared on the 18 May 1926 while swimming in Santa Monica and was presumed drowned. Sightings and ransom notes then began to arrive at the

Hatched, Matched & Despatched

Angelus Temple, where she held her weekly sermons, and five weeks after her disappearance she walked out of the Mexican desert, claiming that she had been kidnapped by three bandits and held in a remote shack.

There were instant suspicions around her story, not least because, despite claiming that she had walked thirteen miles (twenty-one kilometres) in searing desert heat, she appeared to have escaped sunburn and dehydration, and emerged in clean clothes and grass-stained shoes. At a subsequent court hearing, she was accused of spending five weeks holed up with Kenneth Ormiston, a married man who worked at the radio station owned by the Foursquare Church. Other rumours suggested that McPherson had been having an abortion or recovering from plastic surgery, or that it was just a publicity stunt.

Sister Aimee, as she was known, was married three times and cut a glamorous figure, courting Hollywood and making newsreels with Franklin D. Roosevelt and the actress Mary Pickford. Her first visit to the Hall was in April 1926, just before the kidnapping; on the second, in 1928, she came to 'save England', teaming up with the charismatic Welsh evangelist George Jeffreys, founder of the Elim Pentecostal Church, who had already started leading mass baptisms at the Hall that Easter. The press, seeing an attractive woman who behaved more like a movie star than a preacher, and brought her own brand of 'hot-gospelling' to a huge arena, had a field day.

There was also some gentle mockery about the undertaking when, according to the author Ronald W. Clark, an unfortunate misunderstanding occurred:

> One evening she was particularly unlucky, for her demand that those who had seen the light should come forward coincided with the entry into the arena of a small messenger boy, sent to collect an umbrella left during a previous session. Coming down the aisle, he was greeted with a cheer from the white-robed preacher and the joyful words: 'Praise the Lord, you make the thirty-ninth.' With some dismay, but pausing to pick up the umbrella, the lad took to his heels.

Such mass baptisms even made waves overseas – in a piece headlined '10,000 in London See Immersion of 1,000', the *New York Times* reported on 7 April 1928 on The George Jeffrey Massed Baptism Event:

> Loud speakers, floodlights and limelights represented the contribution of science to what otherwise was a huge demonstration of healing by faith. There were fervent shouts of 'Hallelujah!' as the candidates for baptism, the men in

OPPOSITE: Programme
for the Salvation Army's
Funeral Service for
General Bramwell Booth,
23 June 1929.

white flannels and the women in white night dresses, were totally immersed in
the tank, which was decorated to represent the flowing of the River Jordan.

Florence Munday was the first person to be baptised in the Royal Albert
Hall. She claimed that, while being healed by Jeffreys, she had an out-of-body
experience in which she observed her tuberculosis-infected knee being rebuilt.
The following year, the kneecap was medically confirmed as normal. Two more
mass baptisms were carried out by the Elim Church at the Hall, in 1930 and 1938

117. FINAL JOURNEY

The only funeral to be held at the Royal Albert Hall was that of Bramwell
Booth, former General of the Salvation Army, on 23 June 1929. The son of the
Salvation Army's founder William Booth, he had taken over from his father in
1912 but had been deposed after suffering ill health in early 1929. He died on
Sunday 16 June at the age of seventy-three, with his wife and seven children
at his bedside. On the Friday and Saturday following his death, his body lay
in state at the Salvation Army's Congress Hall in Clapton and, as *The Times*
reported, on the Sunday evening 10,000 Salvationists and friends filled the Hall
for the funeral service:

> Very slowly, while the congregation stood, the long procession passed through
> the centre of the building to the catafalque. There it broke up, and those
> who had composed it went to their places in the body of the Hall or on the
> platform. General Higgins, Mrs Booth, and members of her family took their
> places in the centre of the platform immediately above the coffin, and General
> Higgins announced the opening hymn, 'There is a Better World'.

After the service, which lasted three hours, the body was taken to the
International Headquarters of the Salvation Army, in Queen Victoria Street, and
the following day traffic was halted for a procession from the building to Abney
Park Cemetery, Stoke Newington, where Booth was to be buried next to his
parents. Around 40,000 people lined the route with sixteen Salvation Army bands
following the funeral cortège. Florence Booth and her daughters and daughters-
in-law all followed the coffin wearing white sashes, festooned with a large cross
and crown in red.

The hearse was decorated with the Salvation Army shield and bore the words
'In Action Faithful, In Honour Clear', the motto of the Order of Companions of

Hatched, Matched & Despatched

ORDER OF THE

Funeral Services

for

General Bramwell Booth

(Who died at Hadley Wood on Sunday evening, June 16, 1929)

THE ROYAL ALBERT HALL,

Sunday, June 23rd, at 6.30 p.m.

ABNEY PARK CEMETERY,

Monday, June 24th, at 2.30 p.m.

=====

MRS. BRAMWELL BOOTH

with

COMMISSIONER MRS. BOOTH-HELLBERG,

COMMISSIONER CATHERINE BOOTH,

STAFF-CAPTAIN MARIE BOOTH.

COLONEL MARY BOOTH.

LIEUT.-COLONEL AND MRS. BERNARD BOOTH.

MAJOR OLIVE BOOTH.

STAFF-CAPTAIN DORA BOOTH.

STAFF-CAPTAIN AND MRS. WYCLIFFE BOOTH.

MR. AND MRS. BOOTH-CLIBBORN.

also

GENERAL AND MRS. HIGGINS,

The Chief of the Staff and Mrs. MAPP,

and the INTERNATIONAL COMMISSIONERS

GENERAL BRAMWELL BOOTH

ROYAL ALBERT HALL,

KENSINGTON GORE, S.W. 7.

Sunday, 13th July, 1930, at 7 p.m.

Memorial Service

IN REMEMBRANCE OF

SIR ARTHUR CONAN DOYLE, M.D., LL.D.,

KNIGHT OF ST. JOHN OF JERUSALEM,

WHO PASSED TO FULLER LIFE ON MONDAY, 7TH JULY.

Chairman:

GEORGE CRAZE,

President, Marylebone Spiritualist Association.

Organist:

F. ALFORD ARMSTRONG, F.R.C.O.

Under the auspices of
THE MARYLEBONE SPIRITUALIST ASSOCIATION, LTD.,
and
THE SPIRITUALIST COMMUNITY.

RIGHT: A British newspaper covers the death of Sir Arthur Conan Doyle and his funeral at the Hall, 13 July 1930.

FROM THE WORLD'S SCRAP-BOOK:
NEWS ITEMS OF TOPICAL INTEREST.

DESIGNED TO GUARD AGAINST AEROPLANE, AS WELL AS SHIPPING, CASUALTIES:
THE NEW DOVER LIFEBOAT AFTER HER NAMING BY THE PRINCE OF WALES.
The Prince of Wales, in his speech on this occasion, said that several things marked the ceremony as unique in the annals of the lifeboat service; first, the boat herself—the last word in design, workmanship, and material; second, the boat's dual purpose—to guard against casualties to heavy steamship traffic and to aeroplane traffic, a new object of concern to the lifeboat service; third, the boat's name, "Sir William Hillary," recalling that fine English soldier, sailor, scholar, philanthropist, and greatest of lifeboatmen, who was the founder of the Institution in 1824.

A MODEL THAT WILL APPEAR IN THE PORTSMOUTH NAVY WEEK: THE 60 FT.-LONG
REPLICA OF THE "VICTORY," AFTER THE LAUNCHING IN PORTSMOUTH HARBOUR.
The sailing model of H.M.S. "Victory," which, manned by a crew of fourteen officers and a boatswain in the dress of the Trafalgar period, will be one of the attractions of Navy Week at Portsmouth, was launched on July 9 by Miss Doris Drew, daughter of shipwright-officer F. J. Drew, who designed the model "Victory." It is an exact replica of the original, but a quarter of its size, and it will be accurately rigged. Reproduced elsewhere in this number will be found a photograph of some of the capital ships which will take part in the various "Navy Weeks."

THE CREATOR OF "SHERLOCK HOLMES" LAID TO REST IN HIS OWN GARDEN
AT CROWBOROUGH: THE FUNERAL OF SIR ARTHUR CONAN DOYLE.
The spot chosen for his own grave by Sir Arthur Conan Doyle is close to the small wooden hut in which, when the weather permitted, he worked. On the other side is his well-stocked kitchen garden. Mourning was little in evidence at the burial ceremony, which was conducted by the Rev. C. Drayton Thomas, a Wesleyan minister. As the coffin was lowered, Lady Doyle plucked a deep red rose, put it twice to her lips, and let it fall on the grave.

SHOWING THE EMPTY CHAIR, THE SYMBOL OF THE LATE SIR ARTHUR CONAN
DOYLE'S PRESENCE: THE PLATFORM AT THE ALBERT HALL SPIRITUALIST MEETING.
The meeting, at which about six thousand Spiritualists were gathered, was organised by the Marylebone Spiritualist Association, and the Spiritualist Community. The chairman, Mr. George Craze, said that he had been handed a note by Lady Doyle in which she wished to correct the erroneous impression that Sir Arthur's materialised form was expected to appear in the empty chair. "Only those with the God-given extra-sight called 'clairvoyance' would be able to see him."

AT THE IMBER COURT HORSE SHOW AND TOURNAMENT: A MOUNTED
POLICEMAN IN THE MOUNTED FIRING COMPETITION.
Readers will remember that in our issue of June 28 we illustrated a series of feats from the equestrian display and tournament that the Metropolitan Police have been rehearsing. This Show opened before a very large attendance at the Police Sports ground, Imber Court, Thames Ditton, on July 9. There were twenty-five events, and entries numbered over 1000. The prizes were presented by Princess Marie Louise, who was received by Lieut.-Col. P. R. Laurie, Chief of the Mounted Police and director of the show. A bouquet was presented to Princess Louise by a mounted policeman, who caused his horse to bow before her in the most courtly of fashions.

AT THE OPENING OF THE NEW BETHLEM ROYAL HOSPITAL: THE QUEEN WITH THE
PRESIDENT, LORD WAKEFIELD (LEFT OF PHOTOGRAPH), AND DR. J. G. PORTER-PHILLIPS.
On her arrival at the new Bethlem Royal Hospital, at Monk's Orchard, Eden Park, Kent, the Queen was welcomed by Lord Wakefield, the President of the Hospital, and was escorted to the platform by him, and by the Governors, preceded by the beadle. In his speech, Lord Wakefield animadverted to the fact that this was the fourth Royal Hospital of Bethlem which had been built for the maintenance, care, and treatment of those suffering from mental illness. This hospital was founded in 1247, and had probably been associated with the care of mental illness since 1377. Her Majesty is here seen with Lord Wakefield and Dr. J. G. Porter-Phillips, the distinguished alienist, who has been the Physician-Superintendent of Bethlem Royal Hospital since 1914.

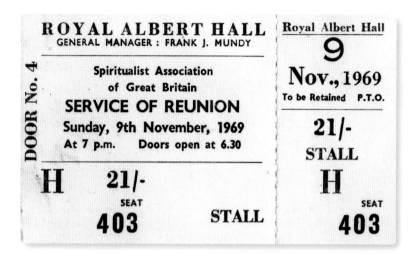

ROYAL ALBERT HALL
GENERAL MANAGER : FRANK J. MUNDY

DOOR No. 4

Spiritualist Association
of Great Britain
SERVICE OF REUNION
Sunday, 9th November, 1969
At 7 p.m.   Doors open at 6.30

H   **21/-**
SEAT
403   **STALL**

Royal Albert Hall
9
Nov., 1969
To be Retained   P.T.O.

21/-
STALL

H
SEAT
403

Ghostbusting

In 1996, as the Hall celebrated
its 125th anniversary, paranormal
investigator Andrew Green spent
the night scrutinising the building. No
ghost appeared, but he did come
across a fluctuation in temperature of
10 degrees Fahrenheit (-12 degrees
Celsius) in a room on the fourth floor,
previously known as the Garden
Room, which he believed to be a
definite sign of paranormal activity.
Green said, 'There was a huge build-
up of static energy in the area near
the organ where Father Willis is said to
be seen. There is no doubt about it –
in my view, there is something strange
going on here.'

Honour, which Booth had been awarded by George V just two months before.

118. LIFE AFTER DEATH

Arthur Conan Doyle was a firm believer in spiritualism, and was involved in many psychic investigations and seances during his lifetime, so it was fitting that a memorial service at the Hall, held by the Spiritualist Society in his honour on 13 July 1930, should receive a message from beyond the grave from the great writer. The extraordinary event, which took place just six days after his death, was hosted by the clairvoyant Estelle Roberts, who was joined on the stage by Lady Doyle and other members of the family, as well as an empty chair marked with the Sherlock Holmes author's name. *Time* magazine reported that, during the evening, Roberts:

> declared five spirits were 'pushing' her. She cried out their messages. Persons in the audience confirmed their validity. Suddenly Mrs Roberts looked at Sir Arthur's empty chair, cried, 'He is here.' Lady Doyle stood up. The clairvoyant's eyes moved as though accompanying a person who was approaching her. 'He is wearing evening clothes,' she murmured. She inclined her head to listen. A silent moment. Her head jerked up. She stared at Lady Doyle, shivered, ran to the widow, whispered. Persons nearby could hear: 'Sir Arthur told me that one of you went into the hut [on the Doyle estate] this morning. Is that correct?' Lady Doyle, faltering: 'Why, yes.' She beamed. Her eyes opened widely. The clairvoyant to Lady Doyle: 'The message is this. Tell Mary [his eldest daughter] …' At this the audience rose in a clamour, and the great organ of the Hall began to peal, the noise drowning out the answer of Mrs Roberts.

Speaking later, Lady Doyle said, 'I am perfectly convinced that the message is from my husband. I am as sure of the fact that he has been here with us as I am sure that I am speaking to you. It is a happy message, one that is cheering and encouraging. It's precious and sacred.' Adrian Doyle, the couple's son, also insisted the message was real: 'The spirit message answers all the tests which my father and mother had agreed upon before his passing. I can only agree with mother that the message is of so intimate a character it cannot be made

The builder of the Hall's organ, 'Father' Henry Willis, who died in 1901, is said to return in ghostly form whenever his handiwork is undergoing restoration. In 1924, workmen reported seeing an old man in a black skullcap walking down some stairs that had been removed years earlier. On hearing their description, the foreman concluded that the spectre was Willis, disturbed by the renovation of his masterpiece. Since then there have been many reports of a sudden chill behind the organ.

In 2018, when asked if he had ever seen signs of Willis, Michael Broadway, the organ's current custodian, recalled: 'I remember the organ builder Clifford Hyatt telling me about this over forty years ago. The tuner, Mr Clay, was making the final visit of the Willis contract before the Harrison & Harrison rebuild in the 1920s. When he got up on to the Great passage board he saw Father Willis there saying, "They shan't take my organ from me." A lovely story, but I haven't seen him. There are many questions I would ask him and hopefully have his approval of the way I look after this instrument. Perhaps he has no reason to be disturbed.'

public even to our closest friends.' Reports at the time suggested the spirit of the suffragette Emily Davison, killed by the King's horse at the 1913 Derby, was also present at the seance.

The memorial service was one of many spiritualist events held at the Hall, including the Centenary Celebration of Modern Spiritualists in March 1948, which saw Roberts and another feted medium, Helen Hughes, impress the audience with messages from loved ones beyond the grave.

119. Tying the Knot

The first wedding to be held at the Hall was staged by ITV's *This Morning* television programme as part of a special edition for its thirtieth anniversary on 4 October 2018. Engaged couples were invited to apply to the show with a forty-second video saying why they should be chosen to have the wedding of their dreams, planned and staged by the channel, to be broadcast live to the nation.

Sarah Roustoby and Shane Maddison, from Hull, were chosen after telling the show they had suffered a series of misfortunes during their thirteen-year relationship. A former Royal Marine, Maddison had been discharged in 2012 after suffering frostbite on a training exercise, and was then diagnosed with an autoimmune disease shortly afterwards. The couple got engaged in 2014 while on holiday in Las Vegas in front of the Planet Hollywood resort and, after three years of fertility treatment, Roustoby gave birth to the couple's daughter Evelyn in August 2017.

This Morning host Holly Willoughby was moved to tears as Roustoby walked down the aisle of the auditorium to the John Legend song 'All of Me', sung by the Kingdom Choir. Roustoby later said that getting married in the Hall was a dream come true. 'It's surreal. It's everything I've ever wanted,' she said. The couple had been officially married the day before the ceremony in the Royal Albert Hall, before saying their vows for a second time in front of their family and friends.

120. A Ghostly Company

Father Willis is not alone in haunting the hall, if other stories are to be believed. The most regular sightings have been of two giggling young ladies in Victorian dresses with cottage-loaf buns and ringlets, who reportedly appeared in the early hours three years running. 'The Girls', as they are now known, were heard by two security staff at two o'clock in the morning on 2 November 1988, passing through the double doors that join the staff canteen to the kitchen corridor. On enquiry to the catering team, they discovered there had been no female staff in the building

RIGHT: Jerry Hall arriving at the Fashion Aid fundraiser in 1985 where Freddie Mercury and Jane Seymour were 'married'.

Hatched, Matched & Despatched

Although the first wedding ceremony at the Hall only took place in 2018, another 'wedding' – this time as part of the Fashion Aid fundraiser in 1985 – had already made headlines. The Live Aid spin-off was organised to raise money for the victims of famine in Africa, and was the largest gathering of fashionistas and style influencers of its time, culminating in a fabulous runway 'wedding' between Queen singer Freddie Mercury and actress Jane Seymour. The 'bride' arrived on stage in a white lace dress tied up with bows, designed by Princess Diana's wedding-gown designers David and Elizabeth Emanuel, and accessorised with a crown of daisies and lilies. She walked down the runway, followed by two page boys, and planted a kiss on Mercury's lips before handing him the massive bridal bouquet. The singer then took off down the runway with the bouquet, throwing blossoms to the delighted crowd.

The huge event, which raised over £1 million, was attended by a host of stars including Boy George, Tina Turner, Grace Jones, Madonna, Ringo Starr, Angelica Houston, George Michael and Jerry Hall, while the catwalk show boasted designs by Armani, Yves Saint Laurent, Calvin Klein and Issey Miyake.

after eleven o'clock. A year later, a concerned porter started following two excitable girls, and raised the alarm after they disappeared at the double doors leading into the kitchen. A full building search found no one, and the terrified porter refused to return to the Hall. In 1990, again at two o'clock in the morning, two girls passed duty manager Rivers Howgill walking towards the kitchen and giggling, but then disappeared. There have been no sightings since.

Some believe the two women could be former inhabitants of Gore House, which occupied part of the site on which the Hall stands. There, society dandy Alfred, Count D'Orsay, lived in sin with Marguerite, Countess of Blessington, stepmother to his former wife, Lady Harriet Gardiner. The Countess spent her late husband's fortune on lavish parties, mainly attended by men, as well by her nieces, the young Misses Powers. Many have speculated that a mysterious basement constructed at the house could have been a brothel, and that 'the Girls' are Countess Blessington and Lady Gardiner, or the Powers.

Other apparitions reported in the Hall are a Victorian couple who sit in one of the boxes; a boy in Victorian clothing spotted leaning over the gallery railings; and a man in white seen walking across the stage at a gig by the comedian Jasper Carrott. A concert-goer from New Zealand once claimed to have seen a military officer on a chestnut horse in the light gantry above the stage, and in January 2004 another visitor to the Hall reported seeing a grey man shrouded in mist who kept appearing then disappearing in the gallery.

One security guard has described an eerie apparition: on opening the door to the lavatories on the gallery floor she found a pulsating grey mass or ball emitting light, which stretched from floor to ceiling. She felt her hair stand on end as if statically charged, and her fingernails felt as if they were made of lead. She was so shaken that she couldn't discuss it with anyone outside the security team for some weeks.

12 THE SILVER SCREEN

The Royal Albert Hall has been the venue for hundreds of film screenings, from 1905 to the present day. As a hall for hire, it is often chosen by film companies as an iconic setting for star-studded premieres, from Bond movies to blockbusters such as *Star Wars: The Last Jedi*. The Hall has also been the star of many a movie, with almost every part of the building, from its iconic balconies and steps to the backstage dressing rooms, making an appearance on the big screen.

121. BATTLE ROYAL

The first film screening at the Hall marked the centenary of the Battle of Trafalgar, on 21 October 1905. *Our Navy*, directed by Alfred John West, included footage of a ninety-two-year-old naval veteran from Portsmouth, who had served under one of Horatio Nelson's captains, showing a young boy around HMS *Victory*. Other clips in the film showed guns from Trafalgar being used by seamen on a contemporary rig.

Religious subjects were popular in the years before the First World War, and the first feature film shown at the Hall was Sidney Olcott's *From the Manger to the Cross*, which sold out for all of its fifty-nine screenings in 1912 and 1913. The movie depicted the life of Jesus, and its lead actor, Robert Henderson-Bland, insisted on wearing a real crown of thorns and carrying a heavy, 15-foot (4.5-metre) cross for its portrayal of the crucifixion. During shooting for the scene in Palestine, Henderson-Bland passed a convent, causing one nun to faint while another rushed out to quench his thirst with a glass of wine. The controversial film prompted the *Daily Mail* to ask 'Is nothing sacred to the film maker?', and the subsequent outcry led to the formation of the British Board of Film Censors.

ROYAL ALBERT HALL

WILLIAM FOX

presents

QUEEN OF SHEBA

A Lavish Spectacle-
Drama

THIS IS THE ONLY HALL WHERE THIS FILM CAN BE SEEN
Commencing Saturday, Jan. 21st, and following d

In January 1922, *The Queen of Sheba* was premiered at the Hall, and caused a scandal over its scantily clad lead, Betty Blythe. The American star, famous as the first actress to appear nude on film, reportedly wore twenty-eight different diaphanous outfits during the film, and at one point sported no more than a string of pearls above the waist. Despite – or perhaps because of – its risqué content, the Prince of Wales, the future King Edward VIII, came to one of the screenings. Sadly, the film was destroyed over time and only a short grainy clip survives.

122. Horrors of War

In 1920, the screening of *Auctions of Souls* (also known as *Ravished Armenia*) caused a political storm. The film centred on the massacre of Armenians in the Ottoman Empire, which left as many as one and a half million people dead, and a female survivor, Arshaluys Mardiganian, played the lead role. The Foreign Office, then in post-war peace talks with Turkey, was nervous about the film's content. The British Board of Film Censors also flagged its concerns, as it was being presented as a documentary rather than entertainment, prompting Scotland Yard to interview the director, Oscar Apfel. Eventually the Foreign Office got cold feet, afraid they could lose a legal challenge if extensive cuts were enforced, and agreed to the film's screening with a few minor alterations. Despite this, it was not granted a certificate by the censors. The decision was to have ramifications later, when Middlesex Council banned cinemas showing any film without a certificate, leading to a legal battle with a local cinema that was flouting the order, which they lost. The ruling led to the Home Office unifying the censorship system across the UK.

123. Orchestral Manoeuvres

The screening of films with a live orchestra is a much-loved part of the Hall's programme today, but the practice actually started one hundred years ago. The first event was the premiere of the Betty Blythe film *Southern Love*, which was accompanied by the London Symphony Orchestra in January 1924. Director Herbert Wilcox transformed the arena into a bullring, covering the floor with sand and sawdust. 'To do this, a new hardwood floor was needed and had to be laid in the twenty-four hours for which I had hired the hall,' he wrote in his autobiography. 'The contractors agreed to do it on time on pain of a heavy forfeit. They succeeded ... A chorus emerged from the tunnels singing the "Toreador Song" from *Carmen*, supported by an orchestra of eighty. Spanish dances took place, and mock bullfights. Twelve

thousand accepted the invitation for the premiere – for which I should explain that there was no charge!'

That same year, the Hall hosted the UK premiere of Fritz Lang's extraordinary two-part fantasy, *Die Niebelungen*, with the London Symphony Orchestra returning to play the score, before the film was shown in 300 theatres nationwide.

124. RUSSIAN REVOLUTION

The era of silent films saw many illustrious screenings at the Hall, including the

Among the Hall's other big-screen appearances are:

The 1944 film *Love Story* features Margaret Lockwood as a dying pianist playing Hubert Bath's 'Cornish Rhapsody' at the Hall.

In *The Seventh Veil* (1945), Ann Todd also plays a pianist performing at the Hall.

In the 1945 adaptation of George Bernard Shaw's play *Major Barbara*, the Salvation Army Band takes to the stage with Rex Harrison and Robert Morley amongst the players – Shaw himself came to the Hall on his birthday to witness the shoot.

In *Give My Regards to Broad Street* (1984), regular Hall visitor Paul McCartney performs '*Eleanor Rigby*' in the auditorium.

Julie Andrews is seen both on stage and in the corridors backstage with Rupert Everett in the weepy *Duet for One* (1986), which sees her playing a violinist.

The 1967 film *Mister Ten Per Cent* has a policeman discovering a construction worker, played by Charlie Drake, curled up asleep in one of the porches, who then explains he is waiting to buy tickets to *Swan Lake* before dancing the highlights for the astonished officer.

In the Dick Clement and Ian La Frenais comedy *Catch Me a Spy* (1971), an incompetent British agent played by Tom Courtenay pursues Marlène Jobert around the Hall.

In the spy thriller *The Ipcress File* (1965), Michael Caine has a confrontation with his quarry on the Hall's south steps, filmed through the glass panes of a phone box placed there for the shooting.

In 1997, the Spice Girls were filmed getting ready in the Hall's dressing rooms for *Spice World: The Movie*.

The 2020 film *Military Wives* recreates the moment in 2011 when the original choir, coached by Gareth Malone, sang at the Festival of Remembrance in front of the Queen.

Misbehaviour (2020), starring Keira Knightley and Gugu Mbatha-Raw, tells the story of the 1970 Miss World protest at the Hall, but the movie's interior scenes were actually shot at the New Wimbledon Theatre.

Jules Verne epic *Michael Strogoff*, directed by Viktor Tourjansky. Over 6,000 people, including ambassadors from fifteen countries, attended the premiere on 6 October 1926. Before the main event, British actors, including John Gielgud, acted out a scene from the Russian epic accompanied by scores of dancing girls and a seventy-five-strong orchestra consisting of members of the Royal Philharmonic and London Symphony orchestras.

With the arrival of sound and increasing numbers of commercial cinemas being built across London, the 1930s saw film move away from the Hall, barely to return for the next six decades.

125. ON CAMERA

Although fewer films were screened in the auditorium in the 1930s, the Hall was beginning to make its own appearances on the big screen. In all, the building has now appeared in over 130 films, including both versions of the Alfred Hitchcock classic *The Man Who Knew Too Much*. The first film, released in 1934, includes a memorable scene in the auditorium when Edna Best's character prevents a planned assassination of a European politician at a concert. Still photographs and footage with actors were shot in the venue, and most of the audience members were then painted onto the photographs, with the final scene being composed through special effects using glass and mirrors, a technique known as the Schüfftan process.

The second version, starring James Stewart and Doris Day, was released in 1956 and remains the most important film shot inside the Hall. This was Hitchcock's only remake of one of his early films, and the new shoot enabled him to spend more time in his favourite London building. This time he shot in colour, using hundreds of extras as concert-goers, and in May and June 1955 the crew spent eleven days in the Hall filming for the dramatic fifteen-minute sequence. Hitch's schedule had a few hitches of its own. An overrun in Marrakesh meant that he arrived late and missed three of the six days for which he had booked the Covent Garden Chorus, who ended up staying past eleven o'clock on the final evening to get the shots. The last four days of filming with the principal cast were cut short because the Hall was booked for evening performances. Eagle-eyed viewers may also notice that the box from which would-be killer Rien (played by Reggie Nalder) falls to his death is none other than the Queen's Box.

Hitchcock had a lifelong love affair with the Royal Albert Hall, having attended Sunday concerts from the age of five. One of the last screenplays he wrote before shifting over to the director's chair was Russian Revolution epic *The Blackguard*, which was first screened at the Hall in 1925. He and wife Alma Reville were frequent visitors, both for concerts and for boxing. His 1927 boxing film *The Ring* was set in the Hall, while in his 1954 classic *Dial M for Murder*, Grace Kelly's wealthy socialite has a ticket for a Royal Albert Hall concert when she is arrested and found guilty of a murder that she did not commit.

On 4 March 4 1971, Hitchcock was the first recipient of a fellowship from what was then the Society of Film and Television Arts. After a speech from the director Richard Attenborough, he was handed his award by Princess Anne, on the stage of his cherished Royal Albert Hall.

The Silver Screen

OPPOSITE: The Royal
World Premiere of James
Bond *Skyfall*, 23 October
2012.

More recent movie appearances include the 1996 movie *Brassed Off*, which culminates at the Royal Albert Hall when the Grimley Colliery Band triumph at the national brass-band championships. The exterior shots for the film, starring Ewan McGregor, Tara Fitzgerald and Pete Postlethwaite, were shot at the Hall, but the interior scenes were actually filmed in Birmingham Town Hall.

Elton John has played many shows at the Royal Albert Hall, including a twelve-night stint of fundraisers for the Elton John AIDS Foundation in 1994, so it's no surprise that the Hall featured in the 2019 biopic *Rocketman*, starring Taron Egerton. Two major concert scenes take place in the Hall, and filming had to take place over just one night, with only twelve hours to get set up, get the shots and get out in between scheduled concerts. The Elgar Room has housed the 'Big Red' piano since 2010, fittingly hand-built for the British star in 2005 for his Red Piano Tour.

126. TOP DOG

In 1996, Walt Disney hired the Hall for the European premiere of *101 Dalmatians*, held in aid of four major charities. Dalmatian markings were projected all over the exterior walls, and spot-shaped confetti rained down inside. Attended by the film's stars Glenn Close, Joely Richardson and Jeff Daniels, the occasion marked the Hall's return to the movie scene and showcased it as a spectacular venue for many movie premieres to come.

127. LICENCE TO THRILL

The Queen was greeted by a unique line-up at the premiere of *Die Another Day* in November 2002 when four James Bonds – Roger Moore, George Lazenby, Timothy Dalton and then 007 Pierce Brosnan – turned up on the red carpet. Halle Berry, who played American agent 'Jinx' Johnson, and Madonna, who sang the theme song, also attended the event, which marked forty years of the superspy franchise.

As a nod to the villain's lair in *Die Another Day*, the interior of the Hall was transformed into an ice palace with the aid of 500 artificial icicles, each twenty feet (six metres) long, along with striking ice-blue lighting. The event raised £500,000 for the Cinema and Television Benevolent Fund.

In 2012, a new Bond, Daniel Craig, attended the world premiere of *Skyfall* in the presence of Prince Charles, with a heavily guarded Aston Martin parked up at the top of the south steps. Three years later, he returned for the premiere of *Spectre*.

ABOVE: The Royal Party
arriving at Royal Film
Performance and World
Premiere of *Die Another
Day*, 18 November 2002.

Above: *Titanic 3D* World
Premiere, 27 march 2012.

128. RINGING THE CHANGES

The screening of films accompanied by live orchestras at the Hall was spectacularly relaunched in 2009 with the sell-out success of *The Lord of the Rings: The Fellowship of the Ring*. Conducted by Ludwig Wicki, the score was played by the London Philharmonic Orchestra, with vocals by the London Voices and the London Oratory School Schola, all of whom had recorded the original soundtrack. A year later, the film's two sequels, *The Two Towers* and *Return of the King*, were also presented with a live orchestra and proved every bit as popular. Since then, a huge range of films have been screened with live orchestras, from *Breakfast at Tiffany's* and *Gladiator* to *E.T. the Extra-Terrestrial* and *The Matrix*.

129. KING OF THE WORLD

James Cameron's box-office behemoth sailed into a new dimension when *Titanic 3D* received its world premiere at the Hall in 2012, one hundred years after the sinking of the ill-fated ship. The audience was limited to 2,700 invited guests and, along with the director, the film's stars Kate Winslet, Billy Zane and Bill Paxton were all in attendance. Three projectors beamed the film from the grand tier onto a huge screen, measuring 69 feet by 29.5 feet (21 metres by 9 metres), and several back-up projectors were on site in case of malfunction. The ship sailed once again in 2015, when James Cameron returned for *Titanic Live* and James Horner's legendary score was played live to a sell-out crowd, before the composer's untimely death later that year.

130. SPACE AGE

On December 2017, the auditorium was transformed into an IMAX cinema for the European premiere of *Star Wars: The Last Jedi*. In the eighteen hours before the screening, a huge team brought in a massive screen, projectors weighing 2,600 lbs (1,200 kg) and a full surround-sound system. Mark Hamill, Daisy Ridley and John Boyega walked the red carpet for the event, along with Princes William and Harry, who actually appear in the film in cameo roles as stormtroopers.

131. AWARDS NIGHT

From 1971 to 1976, the British Academy Film Awards – or BAFTAs – were held at the Hall. They returned once in 1997 and since 2017 have become the official home for the ceremony once again. In 2017, the seventieth BAFTAs were hosted by Stephen Fry, with *La La Land* scooping five gongs: Best Film; Best Director

The Silver Screen

OVERLEAF: The European
Premiere of *Star
Wars: The Last Jedi*, 12
December 2017.

RIGHT: 1997 programme from The 50th (BAFTAs).

OPPOSITE: The EE British Academy Film Awards (BAFTAs), 18 February 2018.

The British Academy Awards 1996

Sunday 13th April and Tuesday 29th April 1997

BRITISH ACADEMY FILM AND TELEVISION ARTS

(Damien Chazelle); Best Actress (Emma Stone); Best Cinematography (Linus Sandgren); and Best Original Music (Justin Hurwitz). Joanna Lumley took over as host the following year.

132. STAR TREKKING

No franchise has more devoted fans that Star Trek, and the Hall has played host to two sold-out conventions for Trekkies, in 1995 and 1996. The first of these, Generations, was the largest Star Trek convention ever staged, with 10,000 fans in attendance, many wearing full costume. The stars of *Star Trek: The Next Generation*, including Patrick Stewart, LeVar Burton, Michael Dorn, Brent Spiner, Jonathan Frakes and Marina Sirtis, took to the Hall's stage for Q&A

sessions over the two days, as well as holding autograph sessions. The rest of the auditorium was awash with memorabilia and limited-edition merchandise, and Patrick Stewart declared it 'an absolutely magnificent event, probably the best ever in the history of Trek'.

A year later the Trekkies were back for Generations II, to mark the show's thirtieth anniversary. Cast members from the original series William Shatner, Walter Koenig and George Takei attended the four-day event over the Easter weekend. The Hall has also featured clips and soundtracks from the Star Trek franchise in its Live in Concert series, including one event in June 2018, where the first ten people to order their tickets in Klingon won two free tickets each.

RIGHT: *Star Trek: The Ultimate Voyage* at the Hall with the London Philharmonic Orchestra, 1 November 2015.

The Silver Screen

JACK SOLOMONS

presents

at the
ROYAL
ALBERT HALL
Monday,
December 2
1946

VINCE
HAWKINS *v.*
Middleweight Champion
of Gt. Britain

JOË
BRUN
(FRANCE)

FINAL ELIMINATING CONTEST
for the
Featherweight Championship
OF GREAT BRITAIN

AL
PHILLIPS *v.*
(ALDGATE)

CLIFF
CURVIS
(SWANSEA)

OFFICIAL
PROGRAMME

2/-

13 A SPORTING CHANCE

Gymnastics was the first sport showcased in the Hall, with a display in 1881 from three hundred athletes from the German Gymnastic Society as part of a military demonstration. Since then, the Hall has hosted sporting events that range from the epic to the bizarre, from legendary boxing matches and table-tennis championships to basketball games and belly barging. The auditorium can be transformed for tennis matches and even indoor marathons, and has hosted squash tournaments, volleyball and netball matches and martial-arts contests.

133. DOCTOR'S ORDERS
Thomas Barnardo, founder of the famous children's homes for orphans, was a firm believer in physical exercise as a route to health and happiness in his young charges. 'Barnardo's Annual Meetings', held at the Hall from 1890, were a chance to demonstrate the success of the fitness regimes in his two London orphanages, and their residents practised for months for the events. Girls from the Barkingside home performed a musical drill, while boys from the Stepney home performed gymnastics to music, showcasing their discipline and physicality. On one occasion, a replica of a ship's rigging was constructed in the arena and the Stepney boys were seen scampering up and down in a demonstration of their fitness and deftness.

134. WORLD'S STRONGEST MAN
The world's first major bodybuilding competition was held at the Hall in 1901, and was judged by athlete and sculptor Charles Lawes and Sherlock

Holmes author Arthur Conan Doyle. The famous writer had become good friends with the event's organiser, the German bodybuilder Eugen Sandow, who had been helping him with body conditioning. Sandow's aim was to promote physical fitness and 'afford encouragement to those who are anxious to perfect their physiques.' The prize was 1,000 guineas and a gold statuette of Sandow worth £500. Sandow's Great Competition was held on 14 September as a fundraiser for injured British troops returning home from the Boer War. Doyle later wrote:

> The Albert Hall was crowded. There were eighty competitors, each of whom had to stand on a pedestal, arrayed only in a leopard's skin. Lawes and I put them up ten at a time, chose one here and one there, and so gradually reduced the number … Finally, we got down to the three winners, but had still to name their order, which was all-important since the value of the three prizes was so very different. The three men were all wonderful specimens, but one was a little clumsy and another a little short, so we gave the valuable gold statue to the middle one, whose name was Murray, and who came from Lancashire.

A lavish champagne banquet followed but when the party was over, Doyle bumped into the winner, gold statuette tucked under his arm, who told him he had no money for a hotel but was waiting until the morning to get a train back to Lancashire.

It seemed to me a monstrous thing to allow him to wander about with his treasure at the mercy of any murderous gang, so I suggested that he should

A Sporting Chance

A Sporting Chance

Opposite: Photograph from the first British indoor marathon, 18 December 1909.

come back with me to Morley's Hotel, where I was residing. We could not get a cab, and it seemed to me more grotesque … that I should be wandering round at three in the morning in the company of a stranger who bore a great golden statue of a nude figure in his arms. When at last we reached the hotel I told the night porter to get him a room, saying at the same time, 'Mind you are civil to him, for he has just been declared to be the strongest man in England.'

On another occasion, in 1889, another display of feats of strength drew a crowd to the Hall, with a less honourable outcome. An appearance by the celebrated French strongman Charles A. Sampson, billed as 'The Strongest Man in the World', ended with a volley of complaints to the Council. Sampson, it turned out, was little more than a vaudevillian showman whose weightlifting feats were achieved through trickery, and who bet members of the audience £100 to challenge him. He was finally exposed when Sandow travelled to Britain to take up the challenges and consistently beat him. More recent weightlifting events include the Strongman Classic.

135. RUNNING IN CIRCLES

The first ever British indoor marathon was run in the auditorium on 18 December 1909, between the Italian athlete Dorando Pietri and the English runner Charles William Gardiner. The previous year, at the London Olympics, Pietri had completed the allotted 26 miles 385 yards in the astonishing time of two hours thirty-eight minutes, but had been disqualified because he received help from the umpires after collapsing from heat and exhaustion. The hugely unpopular decision made him a celebrity, with Queen Mary awarding him a silver

RIGHT: British Empire and American Services Boxing Tournament, 11-12 December 1918.

OPPOSITE: Programme for Professional Boxing Tournament with Muhammad Ali, 19 October 1971.

cup and Irving Berlin writing a song, 'Dorando', which celebrated his run.

The running track built in the arena for the indoor marathon was covered with coconut matting and had a circumference of slightly under ninety yards (eighty-two metres), which meant that the runners need to complete 524 circuits to cover the distance. To 'make the time pass more pleasantly' for the 2,000 spectators, an Italian tenor and military band were laid on. The race began at quarter past eight in the evening, with Gardiner leading most of the way. Dorando, suffering from blisters, changed his shoes after fifteen miles but was eventually forced to retire in his 482nd lap. Gardiner completed the 524 circuits in two hours and thirty-seven minutes to win the £100 purse, while Dorando received £50 for taking part.

In 2009, representatives from the Royal Albert Hall and the Royal Philharmonic Orchestra celebrated the centenary by re-enacting the race, although they didn't attempt to tackle the entire 524 circuits of the arena.

136. IN THE RING

Although applications were made as early as 1893, boxing was initially banned, as it was deemed incompatible with the Hall's constitution and frowned upon by its royal patrons, particularly Edward VII. In 1902, the Council noted the 'King's disapproval of the introduction of professional pugilists into the Royal Albert Hall'. But in the patriotic fervour that followed the First World War, the Hall

MIKE BARRETT presents

Muhammad ALI

TUESDAY, 19th OCTOBER, 1971

THE GREATEST HEAVYWEIGHT OF ALL TIME

ROYAL ALBERT HALL
General Manager :
F. J. Mundy

SOUVENIR PROGRAMME

15p

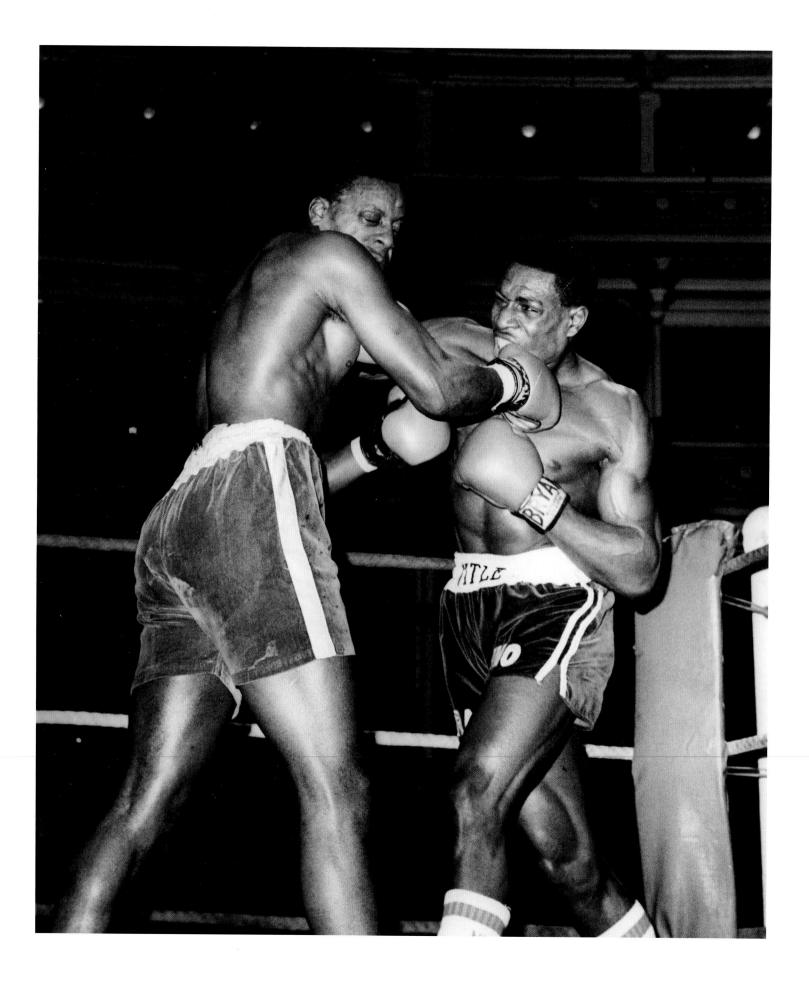

A Sporting Chance

relented and allowed its first real tournament, between sixty-eight servicemen of
the British Empire and American Services in December 1918. George V, who had
ascended the throne eight years earlier, even agreed to hand over the gold trophy
to the winning side, although illness prevented him from doing so on the night.

A report in the Times declared it a triumph for the sport:

> The great game of boxing, soon to be shorn of the vices that have earned
> it so many hostile critics, is being elevated to its rightful plane. The scene
> outside the Albert Hall was almost as wonderful as that which was to be found
> within. Thousands of service men had marched through the rain, spurning the
> omnibuses that were crowded and the taxi-cabs that are now only for the few.
> The queues around the building made a huge star of khaki and blue. Inside
> there is a picture the like of which was surely never dreamed of by fighters
> of other days ... I have just heard an official say to a late arrival that his only
> prospect is that of sitting on the floor. The whole scene is kaleidoscopic. The
> ropes and posts of the ring are bound with flags, a little garish, maybe, but
> the soft shaded curtains of the tiers of boxes tone everything into harmony.
> The fever of fighting is in the air – good fighting, clean fighting, and all for the
> honour of the game.

The event paved the way for a series of twelve boxing matches between
December 1919 and November 1920 under Championship conditions, for gold
trophies or cups, but not for 'prize money, purse, side-stake or wager'. The
French pugilist Georges Carpentier fought three exhibition rounds, appropriately
enough on Boxing Day 1919. Shortly after, on 13 January 1921, the Prince of
Wales, the future Edward VIII, who was a great boxing fan, sat ringside to
watch the American Pete Harman beat the Welsh fighter Jimmy Wilde in the
seventeenth round.

Prize fights for cash were finally allowed in the Hall in 1925, although betting
during bouts was banned and anyone seen to be flouting the ban was ejected.
Boxing fans loved the venue's layout, which ensured that no spectator far from
the ring, as well as necessitating a smaller ring and delivering a harder fight. Over
the next seventy years, huge names in the sport appeared at the Hall, including
Henry Cooper, who fought six times between 1952 and 1964, and Frank Bruno,
who appeared in the ring sixteen times. Muhammad Ali boxed eight exhibition
rounds on 19 October 1971, and made his final appearance at the Hall with a
further five rounds of exhibition boxing on 1979 in Farewell to London: The

Magic of Ali. 'Prince' Naseem Hamed fought Juan Polo Perez at the Hall on 1 July 1995, while Lennox Lewis appeared no fewer than seven times.

Another notable tournament saw the notorious Kray twins, Reggie and Ronnie, fighting on the same bill as older brother Charlie on 11 December 1951. Sports journalist Colin Hart remembers watching amateur matches at the Hall in the 1960s and 1970s:

> It could be a dangerous place sitting ringside at the Albert Hall, because of the crowd. Don't get me wrong, there was no crowd trouble or rioting but in the '60s and '70s there was a thing called 'nobbins'. If the crowd were happy with how the men performed, to supplement their money, they would throw money in the ring. Coins, mainly. They threw them from far away, often half-crown pieces … If they landed on your head, they'd split it open!

Boxing took a twelve-year break from the Hall from 1999, when residents' complaints led to the licence being revoked. However, the decision was overturned in 2011, and the sport's return was marked with a charity contest between the UK Armed Forces and the US Armed Forces in a nod to the first historical tournament of 1918.

Championship boxing made its return on 28 April 2012, with a line-up including some of the best British boxers, including Billy Joe Saunders and Tony Hill. In September 2019, Nicola Adams and Maria Salinas became the first female boxers to fight at the Hall. The British star held on to her WBO flyweight title in the first world-title fight at the venue since Marco Antonio took on Paul Lloyd in 1999, but the controversial draw proved to be Adams's swansong – she announced her retirement two months after the match.

137. Boxing Clever

The loading bay was the setting for the ultimate clash of brains and brawn, when a chessboxing tournament was staged there in October 2012. Competitors play four minutes of speed chess on a chessboard in the centre of a ring between three-minute boxing rounds, an undertaking that combines the strategy, tactics and punching-power of both activities, in an intense physical and mental mix-up.

First reported in 1978, the sport has a growing fan base, and the four bouts were part of the Hall's commitment to provide new and innovative programming and unique experiences for all. A capacity crowd witnessed some of the best chessboxers, including Chris Levy and Sean Mooney, surrounded by graffiti art depicting some of the legendary performers who have graced the Hall's main stage.

138. WRESTLING

Although boxing was banned, championship wrestling was allowed at the Hall as early as 1904, when the Estonian strongman George Hackenschmidt defeated the American champion Tom Jenkins for a purse of £2,500. The match was only permitted as long as it was 'free from anything vulgar or incompatible with the dignity and reputation of the Hall, and that the competitors would be properly clothed so that there would be nothing of the semi-nude in the entertainment'. In 1921, the Duke of York, Prince Albert, gave the sport a royal seal of approval by handing out the prizes at the Metropolitan Police Amateur Boxing and Wrestling Competition. The sport's popularity really took off from the 1950s to the 1980s, with sell-out crowds flocking to seven or eight tournaments each year. Big names in wrestling who appeared at the Hall include Mick McManus, Jack Dempsey, Jackie Pallo, Giant Haystacks and Big Daddy.

Celebrated artist Peter Blake went to the monthly tournaments with his mother and aunt throughout the 1960s and 1970s. 'We'd stand in the corners [by the ring]. The very first fight I saw – I can remember absolutely clearly –was between Mick McManus and a little Jewish wrestler called Al Lipman, whose speciality was that when the other wrestler came towards him, he jumped out of the ropes and ran away. I saw some great fights there. I used to go with my sketchbook and sit up in the Gods. My hero was Mick McManus and then later Kendo Nagasaki.'

Nagasaki, real name Peter Thornley, was one of the most feared and hated wrestling stars, and he remembers one lady who let her feelings get the better of her:

> One night I was coming out of a wrestling ring and there was this lady in her late thirties or early forties standing in the aisle, blocking my way. I thought, 'She's just a woman, I'm in no danger here.' So I marched up ... Suddenly this handbag came up and hit me on the side of the face, knocking me to the floor. I jumped up, grabbed the handbag, ripped it open and half a wall brick came out! Quite a shock!

Prince Philip, Duke of Edinburgh, attended a charity tournament in May 1963, which raised £10,000 for His Royal Highness's Award Scheme. He entered the ring and met the wrestlers before the fights and again to present a trophy to Hungarian-born wrestler Tibor Szakacs after his defeat of the New Zealander John da Silva.

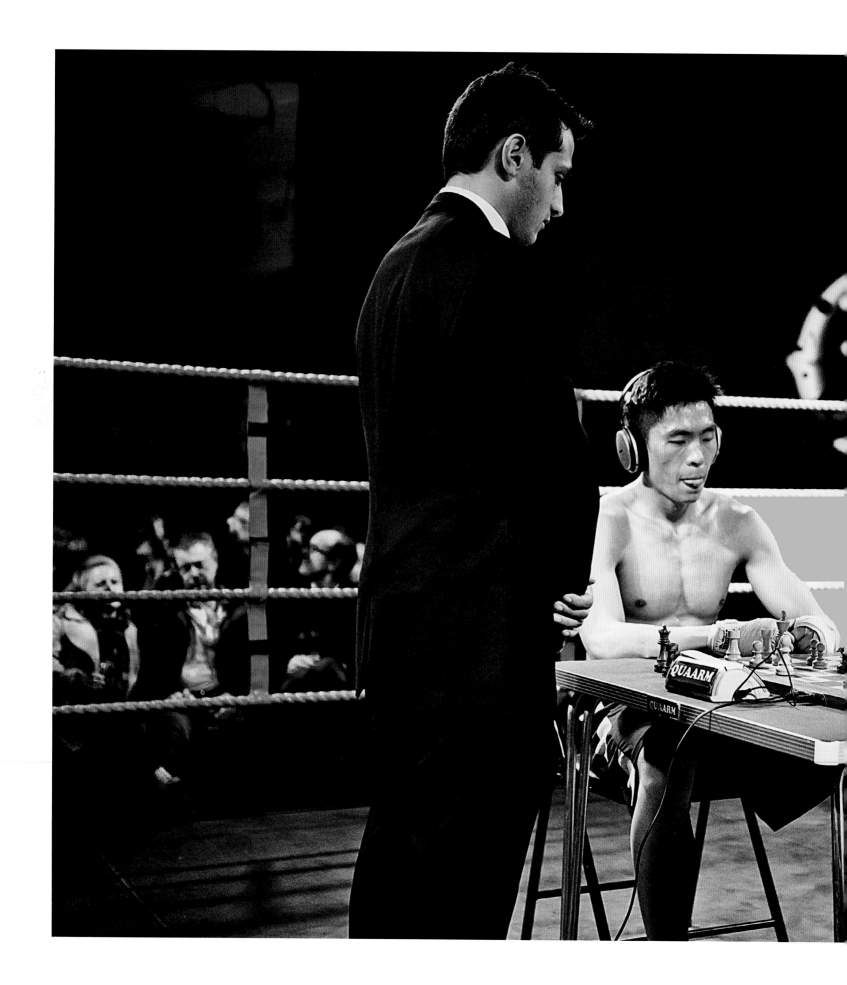

A Sporting Chance

LEFT: Sean Mooney and Bryan Woon during the Chessboxing event in the Loading Bay of the Royal Albert Hall, 10 October 2012.

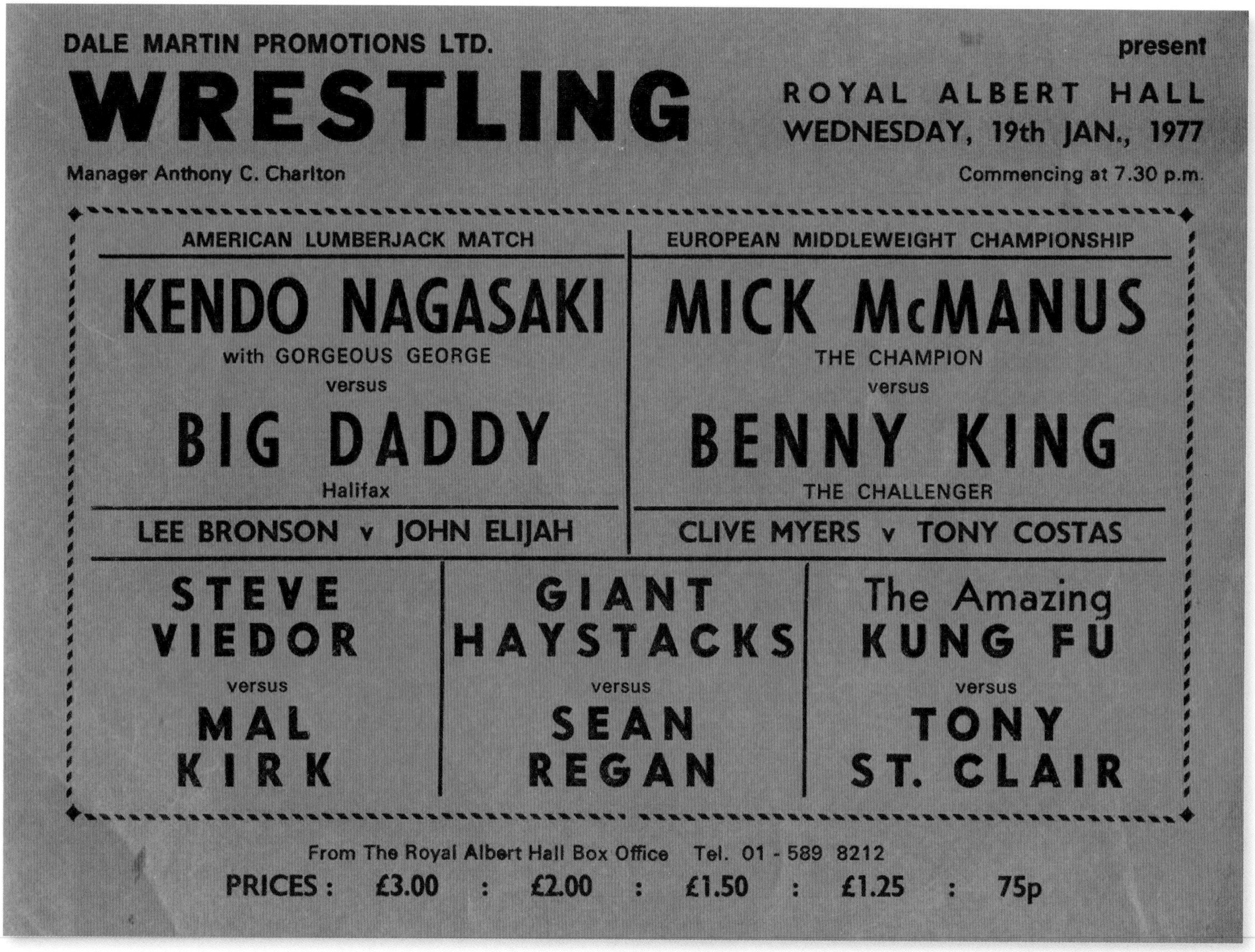

ABOVE: Handbill
from Dale Martin's
International Professional
Wrestling Tournament,
The Wrestling
Spectacular, 19 January
1977.

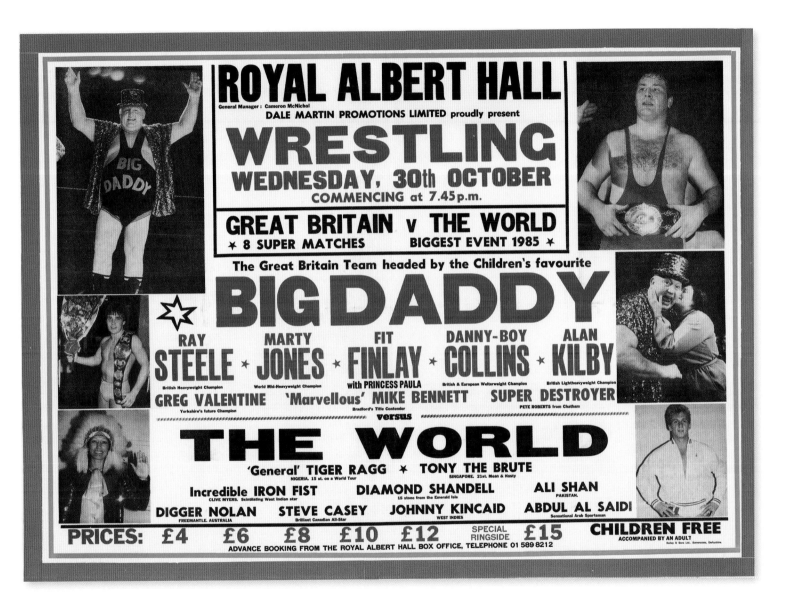

ABOVE: 1980s poster of
wrestling held at the Royal
Albert Hall, 30 October
1985.

October 1991 saw the arrival of the World Wrestling Federation's Battle Royal at the Hall. Some of the biggest names in wrestling took part, including the Undertaker, Big Boss Man and Earthquake, and the event culminated in the 'battle royal', with twenty wrestlers piling into the ring to be eliminated one by one by being thrown over the top rope. British Bulldog claimed victory after defeating his final opponent, Typhoon.

139. Heavy Duty

The first Sumo-wrestling tournament staged outside Japan in the sport's 1,300-year history was staged at the Royal Albert Hall in October 1991 as part of the Japan Festival. Instead of the conventional fifteen-day event, the Grand Sumo Tournament was cut down to five days for UK audiences.

Before each tournament, it is traditional for the yobidashi, or ring attendant, to spend three days building the sacred dohyo (the wrestling ring) from straw and clay, which is traditionally sourced from the banks of the Arakawa River that flows through Tokyo. For the UK tournament, the correct clay was tracked down to a quarry near Heathrow, while a huge drum and the ceremonial canopy, the yokata, were both shipped in from Japan. The event was a sell-out, with the most expensive seats being the cushions placed on the floor around the dohyo.

The tournament began with a dohyo-matsuri, a ceremony to cleanse and bless the ring, conducted by the chief referee. The top forty wrestlers, known as rikishi, competed, including two yokozuna (grand champions) – Asahifuji Seiya and Hokutuomi Nobuyoshi. But the main attraction was the Hawaiian wrestler Konishiki Yasokichi, the heaviest sumo ever, nicknamed the Dump Truck, who weighed in at thirty-seven and a half stone (238.25 kg).

Before the wrestlers arrived, the backstage lavatories were weight-tested, chairs reinforced and extra-large showers fitted. Michele Finley, former executive assistant at the Hall, remembers meeting these sporting giants backstage: 'That was an experience. You'd walk around in the day and you would see all the wrestlers walking down the corridors, and they were huge. They stayed locally at the Royal Garden Hotel, and they had to reinforce all the beds there to carry them.'

140. Yoga Gurus

The Women's League of Health and Beauty put on the first of many demonstrations of its fitness routines on 25 April 1931. Set up just a year earlier by Mary Stack and her daughter Prunella, who had seen the benefits of yoga while living in India, the group aimed to improve the health of women of all classes by providing cheap exercise classes across the country, charging just a sixpence a time. They introduced many of the fitness techniques still popular today, including pilates, aerobics, dance exercise and yoga.

The first of the League's annual celebrations at the Hall saw five hundred women in its snazzy uniform of a white sleeveless blouse and black shorts, all performing a display of exercises to music. Routines included 'Exercises for Central Control', 'Exercises for Circulation' and even 'Combined Exercises for Feet', and prizes were awarded to winners of the Graceful Walking Competition.

SUMO

THE GRAND TOURNAMENT

The Royal Albert Hall
9·13 October 1991

A Sporting Chance

A Sporting Chance

OPPOSITE: Handbill from
Pro-Celebrity Tennis
Tournament, 22 June
1984.

OVERLEAF: Aegon
Masters Tennis
Tournament, 3 December
2009.

Throughout the years, the group, now known as the Fitness League, has returned for anniversary celebrations including its golden and diamond jubilees in 1980 and 1990 respectively, as well as its eighty-fifth birthday in 2015.

Since then, yoga has been a regular fixture at the Hall, with Sahaja Yoga events in the main auditorium from 1993 to 2000; a mass yoga class with instructor Annie Clarke in 2018 ahead of that year's Champions Tennis event; and regular classes for both children and adults in the Elgar Room today.

141. Royal Court

Tennis has become the Hall's most regular sporting fixture since debuting with two tournaments in 1970 – the Rothmans International Tennis Tournament for men, and the Dewar Cup for both men and women. British favourite Virginia Wade dominated the women's Dewar Cup, winning seven times between 1968 and 1976, five of these victories taking place at the Hall. Rod Laver triumphed at the 1971 Rothmans tournament, while the 1974 winner was Björn Borg, who was just seventeen at the time.

In order to accommodate a full-sized tennis court, the Great Floor was initially installed for each tournament, but the carpet laid on the boards slowed the ball down, making the first tournaments painfully long. The updated false floor, the Exhibition Floor , covering the first five rows of the stalls, was installed for the first time to solve the problem. Today, transforming the Hall into a court is an overnight job, with thirty workers taking out the 1,500 chairs from the arena and installing the replacement floor.

From 1978 to 1988, the annual Wightman Cup between teams from the UK and the US was played at the Hall every second year. The first visit of the three-day competition for women in 1978 saw a British team that included stars Virginia Wade and Sue Barker defeating the equally star-studded American team, led by Billie Jean King, Chris Evert and Pam Shriver.

But it's not just professional players who have swung a racquet in the auditorium. Bruce Forsyth, Bobby Moore and Terry Wogan were among the legends who played in the Amstrad Pro-Celebrity Tennis Tournament, in aid of the Muscular Dystrophy Group, in 1989. Since 2015, the Hall has hosted the biannual Champions Tennis event, which mixes world-class matches from past champions such as Greg Rusedski, Tim Henman and Martina Hingis with entertainment. The Masters Tennis Tournament is also staged in the Hall every second year, and in 2018 specially trained dogs provided by the charity Canine Partners were used to retrieve the balls.

14 PUBLIC ENGAGEMENT

The Royal Albert Hall has been a registered charity since 1967, held in trust for the nation's benefit, with the aim of promoting the arts and sciences and preserving and enhancing the Grade I listed building. All profits made by the Hall, therefore, either go towards maintenance and upgrades of the building, or on its Education and Outreach Programme. Throughout the year, the Hall provides performances at day centres and hospices, music events for all ages and curriculum-based workshops for school groups. In addition, the Hall has hosted events for numerous charitable partners, including Barnardo's, the Red Cross, Save the Children, the Blue Cross, Fashion Aid, the Teenage Cancer Trust, Bloodwise, Children in Need and many more.

Flo Schroeder, the Hall's senior Education and Outreach manager, says, 'Our Education and Outreach programme is essential to everything that the Royal Albert Hall represents as a venue and as an institution. We were established with a founding mission to provide a "Central Hall for the arts and sciences" that would nurture a love of music and a sense of community, and we remain true to Prince Albert's vision.'

142. STORY TIME
Engagement at the Royal Albert Hall starts from the age of zero, with regular storytelling and music sessions for under fours being held in one of the historic ground-floor porches of the Hall. As well as weaving entertaining tales,

Right: Programme for Music for Youth's Schools Prom 1995, 6-8 November 1995.

Public Engagement

storytellers such as Paul Rubinstein and Samantha Sutherland also use singing,
games and musical instruments to keep the babies and toddlers enthralled, and to
get them moving, encouraging interaction with their parent or carer. 'Music gets
them communicating with their grown-ups, it gets them being part of a group,
it gives them confidence, and it's also great fun,' says storyteller Becky Dixon.
'When you see the children start dancing, moving and smiling, when something
just speaks to them and the room begins to move all as one, it's a beautiful
experience.'

Laura Edralin, who works at the Hall, took her son Maxwell, then sixteen
months old, to a session and says he loved every second: 'Maxwell was gripped and
happily singing, dancing, stamping and doing all the hand shapes and signs as Paul
led us through. It ended with a paper-tearing game, simple enough for even the

littlest and magical enough for the older tots, and when we threw all the "confetti" in the air, I realised that even the most tired of adults were gasping with delight!'

143. Supporting Schools
Children both in and out of the classroom have benefitted from the Education and Outreach Programme, whether through a special performance held at the Hall, or an event at their school. The innovative Discover series sees talented music workshop leaders taking to the classroom to teach such lessons as 'Discover Music and Maths' and 'Discover Music and Science', which engage Key Stage 2 and 3 children in difficult subjects through the power of music. Held at the Hall, the Evolution project delivered in partnership with Rolls Royce aims to get Year 5 and 6 pupils interested in design and engineering, with teams designing and building models based on the Cirque du Soleil set. Other events include dedicated school matinee concerts, including the ever-popular Classical Spectacular, which introduces children to a full symphony orchestra, integrating incredible lighting and lasers to create an unforgettable experience. In addition, Albert's Band – the Hall's resident ensemble, which draws on a pool of hundreds of professional musicians – delivers a series of free school workshops in local primary schools, while the Education and Outreach Programme offers free instrumental lessons for forty children each year to build a legacy for this project.

144. Young Musicians
As part of its commitment to promote music for young people, the Hall has a long-running partnership with the youth-arts charity Music for Youth, which puts on two Primary Prom concerts each year. Young musicians and youth orchestras provide the music and 9,000 tickets are given away each year to primary schools. In addition, a strategic partnership with the Tri-borough Music Hub is another key part of our Education and Outreach Programme, bringing music to 5,000 pupils in fifty schools across the London Borough of Hammersmith and Fulham, the Royal Borough of Kensington and Chelsea and the City of Westminster.

In 2015, the partnership commissioned *Seven Seeds*, a new piece by composer John Barber and writer Hazel Gould inspired by the Greek myth of Persephone. Written with the input of children across the three boroughs, it premiered at a special concert involving over 1,200 young singers and an orchestra comprised of musicians from Albert's Band, Aurora Orchestra and Southbank Sinfonia, as well as students from the Royal College of Music and the Royal Academy of Music.

More recently, a two-year project brought thousands of young musicians together to contribute to a composition exploring how music gives everyone a voice and provides a soundtrack to all lives. Written by up-and-coming composer Charlotte Harding, the newly commissioned musical *Convo* gave young people from across the boroughs the chance to perform on the Hall's famous stage, with over 1,000 young instrumentalists and singers taking part, conducted by Ben Palmer.

145. MUSIC AS THERAPY

In partnership with the music charity Nordoff Robbins, the Education and Outreach team hold weekly music-therapy sessions that can transform the lives of children and adults with a whole range of disabilities and special educational needs. Music therapy has been proven to benefit people with living with autism, dementia, mental-health problems, learning disabilities and social, emotional and behavioural difficulties, encouraging confidence and communication. Set up in 1970 by American composer and pianist Paul Nordoff and special-education teacher Clive Robbins, the charity now trains its own music therapists and provides therapy sessions in schools, care homes and hospices around the country.

Neil Warnock, chairman of the charity, says that the weekly sessions at the Royal Albert Hall provide a vital service for vulnerable children and adults:

> The Trustees of the Hall have recognised, through being at our functions, that music and therapy is something that co-exists, and that's why they have been generous enough to give us rooms for music therapy. The Hall is part of the community and those that need Nordoff Robbins' music therapy can now receive it at the iconic Royal Albert Hall. How wonderful is that?

146. INSPIRING CAREERS

The Albert Sessions concert series enables young, world-class artists who haven't headlined at the Hall before to showcase their talent on the main stage, while also attracting younger audiences through lower ticket prices. As well as their headline concert, the artists host inspirational workshops and experiences for young people across all musical genres in collaboration with the Hall's Education and Outreach team. Artists who have featured in the Albert Sessions include Chvrches, Marina and the Diamonds and Michael Kiwanuka. In 2017, Nigerian singer Wizkid became the first Afrobeats star to headline at the Hall when he staged a concert in aid of the Evening Standard Dispossessed Fund's Grenfell Tower appeal.

RIGHT: Albert Sessions:
An Evening With Alison
Balsom, 13 October
2014.

Public Engagement

During the 2013 Albert Sessions, budding violinists were given the chance to have one-to-one lessons with the legendary Nicola Benedetti in five workshops over three days. The following year Jake Bugg ran two sessions with young singers exploring, coaching and rehearsing one of his own songs, before giving some of them the once-in-a-lifetime opportunity of joining him on stage during his own concert in the auditorium. Other acts who have hosted Albert Sessions workshops include Emeli Sandé, Sigma, Alison Balsom, Foals, Lianne La Havas and country-music star Kacey Musgraves.

Rap star Kano, who hosted a workshop in November 2019, believes the Albert Sessions are an amazing initiative:

> I really enjoyed it. I think it's a great thing, just to be able to give back. People think giving back is about money but, no, it's also about inspiring and giving some of your time to hear where they're at and what they're interested in. Maybe some of us are interested in the same thing and if it's music production, we can show you how we do it and what goes into a creating a song that you can one day perform at a building like this. It's just a beautiful exchange and I'm really thankful for the opportunity to do that.

A large part of the Hall's charitable and outreach work is carried out by members of the in-house ensemble Albert's Band. Formed in 2009, Albert's Band is a versatile and highly skilled group of professional musicians who put on bespoke performances and workshops for all ages, both at the Hall and out in the community. The resident ensemble for the Hall's extensive Education and Outreach Programme, they perform at everything from the Albert's Band Presents half-term family concerts in the Hall's Elgar Room, to free Songbook sessions in care homes and hospices, to festivals around the UK.

Albert's Band by Numbers

Around 250 musicians, covering many musical styles including Orchestral, Jazz, Folk, Opera, Rock and Pop

Over 600 concerts and performances

Over 300 workshops

Engaged with over 100,000 people over ten years

The Hall also runs Careers Master Classes, supporting young people in the arts and giving them a unique insight into what it means to work in the world's busiest venue. As part of the scheme, the Elgar Room recently hosted a Young Producers course, during which young people between eighteen and twenty-five planned and staged their own events. Savannah Simms, who took part in the scheme, said, 'It's been great. We are all different people, we come from different places, we all want different things for the future but the fact that we are all working under one roof to create something bigger and better is just incredible.'

147. Teenage Cancer Trust Workshops

The Royal Albert Hall has been hosting annual gigs in aid of the Teenage Cancer Trust since 2000. In addition, since 2005 the Hall has worked with the charity to put on the Teenage Cancer Trust Music Workshops for young people living with the disease. These involve a tour of the building and a songwriting session when the teenagers get to play instruments, write songs and form new friendships. The event enables the guests to share their personal experiences and allows them to forget about the traumas of treatment and focus on being a teenager again.

After the workshop, they enjoy an evening meal, a ticket to that evening's concert and hotel accommodation, and they often get to meet the stars of the show. In 2017, Busted members Matt Willis, Charlie Simpson and James Bourne were in the audience to watch the workshop performance before supporting Ed Sheeran's gig that evening, and in 2019 Locksmith from Rudimental dropped in. The Stereophonics frontman Kelly Jones even joked about the kids stealing riffs from his song 'Maybe Tomorrow' when he made a surprise visit in 2015: 'They nick a few of the chords that we had in a song, put them in a different order and then write a new song – it's pretty much what I do most days!'

148. Senior Sing-a-longs

At the other end of the age scale, the Hall launched its Royal Albert Hall Songbook project in 2013, to bring music to elderly people in the nation's care homes and hospices. Members of Albert's Band lead hour-long singalongs in the homes, performing music by the Beatles, Frank Sinatra and Dame Vera Lynn, giving almost 3,000 people a year a chance to sing, dance and share in a life-enhancing experience. Yi Xu, a carer at the Forrester Court home in Paddington, said, 'Our residents thoroughly enjoyed singing and dancing together, and afterwards had lots of talk about the old songs and memorable events in the past.'

Public Engagement

On her one-hundredth birthday in March 2017, Dame Vera Lynn praised the
scheme saying:

> I'm proud and pleased to be associated with the Royal Albert Hall Songbook,
> which brings live music to those who might not otherwise be able to take part
> in it, and shares some of my own best-loved songs, including 'We'll Meet
> Again' and 'The White Cliffs of Dover'. On my hundredth birthday, it's so
> lovely to know that these songs which mean so much to me continue to be
> listened to and enjoyed, and that the Royal Albert Hall can be enjoyed by
> elderly people regardless of money or mobility.

Dame Vera has performed at the Hall fifty times throughout her illustrious
career, appearing first at the Pitman's College Prize Giving and Concert in
1937, and most recently at the Dekho! Forty-Ninth and Final Burma Reunion
in 1995.

149. DEMENTIA SCREENINGS

Living with dementia can leave people isolated and feeling unable to enjoy
the arts in a way that they might have done in the past. With that in mind, the
Hall runs regular dementia-friendly film screenings in the Elgar Room, where
guests can relax in a comfortable environment while watching classic films such
as *Meet Me in St Louis*, *Easter Parade*, *The Wizard of Oz* and *Calamity Jane*,
and also more recent titles including *La La Land*. Measures to help provide the
perfect environment include dementia-friendly training to front of house staff, a
quiet room for those who may need to leave the Elgar Room, dementia-friendly
signage and a reduced capacity of forty. Lighting levels are also kept at fifteen
per cent to avoid complete blackout, which might cause distress.

Other events tailored to the elderly and those living with dementia include
the regular Tea Dances, which provide a chance to socialise and dance to music
from Albert's Big Band, and the Afternoon Coffee Club, a relaxed, informal way
to meet others and chat while enjoying live-music entertainment. Flo Schroeder
said, 'As the age of the UK population increases, there has been an ever-growing
understanding of the impact that participating in the arts, and perhaps especially
in music, can have on our health and well-being.'

150. A HAND OF FRIENDSHIP

In keeping with Prince Albert's vision of a venue to be enjoyed by everyone,

the Hall launched its Friendship Matinees in 2013. These afternoon events are
open to people from all age groups who are supported by charity, community or
voluntary groups, and who would otherwise not come to the Hall. The initiative
gives them the opportunity to see world-class performances at £5 per ticket.
The series kicked off with a celebration of John Barry's movie themes, sung by
Alison Jiear and Lance Ellington with the Royal Philharmonic Orchestra. James
Bond themes from such films as *Diamonds Are Forever* and *Goldfinger* were
mixed in with other unforgettable classics from *Dances with Wolves*, *Out of Africa*
and *Midnight Cowboy*. Since then, these annual concerts have included Best
of Broadway, Symphonic Queen and Abbaphonic, as well as special Christmas
performances.

After one Friendship Matinee, Georgia Bowers from the London Bubble
Theatre wrote: 'Our participants really did enjoy it and for many of them
it was the first time that they had attended an event at the Hall. In fact, our
eldest member Dolly, who's ninety, commented that it was not only her first
visit to the Royal Albert Hall but also her first experience of a live orchestra!
So thank you for providing our group with a set of lovely new memories and
experiences.'

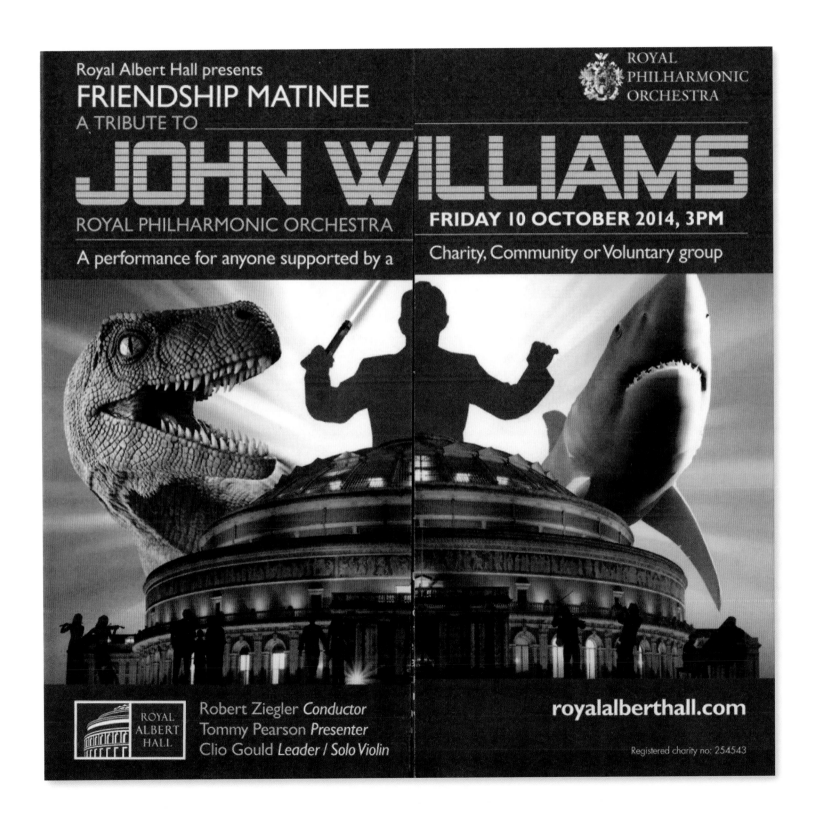

BELOW: The original
trumpet played at the 1871
opening ceremony of the
Royal Albert Hall.

BELOW: The original
trumpet played at the 1871
opening ceremony of the
Royal Albert Hall.

15 THANKS FOR THE MEMORIES

Over the last 150 years, millions of people have passed through the doors of the Royal Albert Hall, from royalty and showbusiness legends to the cooks, cleaners and maintenance workers who keep the fabric of the building shipshape.

In 2017, the Hall launched an oral history project, Albert Speaks, with the support of the Blavatnik Family Foundation, as well as starting the Royal Albert Hall '150 Memories' project. Hundreds of memories from audience members, staff and artists have now been recorded for posterity and launched on a new digital platform to be enjoyed by all who love this iconic building. In addition, our archives hold numerous volumes of visitors' books, with comments from many of the thousands of performers who have graced the stage. Here, a few of the people who have visited or worked at the Hall share their thoughts and memories.

GLASS HOUSE

The domed roof is a beautiful and much-loved architectural feature for those who visit the Hall but, for staff, working under glass presents its own problems. In the height of summer, the auditorium can get exceptionally warm. Michele Finley, the Hall's former executive assistant, remembers how one clever staff member made perfect use of the conditions:

> When I first joined at the Hall we had various unusual employees, not in person but in title. The Hall employed a glazier. His job was to look after the glass in the domed roof. He'd see if any of it needed tending to and he grew tomatoes up there. He probably spent as much time tending the tomatoes as the glass in all honesty!

'QUEEN' ELIZABETH

Eric Clapton, the Hall's most prolific living headliner, remembers a very special occasion when he met a Hollywood legend at one of his own shows:

I was told that Elizabeth Taylor was coming. This was when she was hanging out with Michael Jackson and she was in a very diva state of mind. They said, 'Would you like to meet her?' and I said 'Of course.' I assumed she would be brought to the green room and instead the guy came and got me from my dressing room and said, 'She's ready to see you now, just follow me.' We went to another dressing room and she was in there. The bouquets were her favourite flowers, the dressing room had been painted her favourite colour, which I think was lilac, and all of this to prepare for her coming. I was visiting

A Homecoming

A very special memento returned to the Hall in May 2016 when a trumpet that had been played at the opening ceremony was handed in – after 145 years. The trumpet, made by a London-based company called Butler, bears the inscription 'This instrument played by Mr C Bailey at the opening of the Royal Albert Hall, London, 1871' along with the maker's initials.

The brass instrument, one of the few physical objects the archives contain from the ceremony, would have played an important role in the concert as part of the trumpet fanfare heralding Queen Victoria's arrival to the Hall and announcing its opening. It was seized by Thames Valley Police from a property in Buckinghamshire in 2015, and passed on to the Police Evidence Management Unit in Milton Keynes. There, Thames Valley Police support worker Andy Angus spotted its significance, and took it upon himself to deliver the trumpet personally to the Hall, an act that definitely deserves a fanfare.

Elizabeth in HER dressing room at my own show. That's the funniest thing I've ever experienced. It's the kind of place where you can get away with that, and there's a humour to it that belongs to the building.

CREATING LEGENDS

In 1906, visionary speech-and-drama teacher Elsie Fogerty founded the Central School of Speech Training and Dramatic Art in the West Theatre at the Royal Albert Hall, now known as the Elgar Room. Long before universities taught drama, Fogerty argued that theatre should be a degree subject. She offered courses in elocution, speech therapy, debating and public speaking, as well as recitation, fencing, dancing and drama to help would-be actors hone their skills. Laurence Olivier, Judi Dench, Harold Pinter, Peggy Ashcroft, Vanessa Redgrave,

RIGHT: Advert for the
Central School of Speech
and Drama c. 1906.

SCHOOL OF

DRAMA, SPEECH TRAINING and PHYSICAL EDUCATION.

MISS ELSIE FOGERTY, Lecturer to
Teachers under the Education Depart-
ment of the L.C.C., Roedean School, etc., etc.
SESSION NOW OPEN.

Dramatic, Elocution, Dancing and Voice Training Classes at the
ROYAL ALBERT HALL

The Course includes :—
Recitation. - The treatment of all forms of Speech Defects.
Public Speaking and Debating.
The School of Dramatic Art, under the Presidency of Mr. F. R. Benson.
Training Course for Teachers of Speech and Voice.
A special section of the school is devoted to the training of students who wish to fit themselves
for posts as teachers of Elocution and Speech Training. There is now a wide demand for this
work, and centres have been established in Liverpool, Manchester, Edinburgh, Newcastle,
St. Andrews, Nottingham, Malvern, etc.
SINGLE CLASSES may be taken in
Elocution and Drawing Room Recitation. Dancing. Rehearsal.
Fencing. Voice Training and Physical Exercises.
Debating and Public Speaking (Miss Elsie Fogerty).
For Course and Fees and other particulars apply to—
MISS ELSIE FOGERTY, 29 Queensberry Place, South Kensington.
Arrangements are made to board Students coming from the country.

Joss Ackland and Cicely Berry are among those who learned their trade on the
West Theatre stage, before the Central School moved to larger premises at the
Embassy Theatre in Swiss Cottage in 1957.

Butterflies actress Wendy Craig and *The Archers* legend Patricia 'Paddy'
Greene also studied under Fogerty at the Hall, and they recall the school's
unusual techniques in a recent conversation for the Albert Speaks project:

Paddy: We were raring to go when we first joined of course. But they said,
'Lie on the floor' and what they were doing was relaxing … It was hard work
relaxing! They were rebuilding us you see. We didn't realise at the time, but we
had the best voice teacher ever called Cicely Berry.
Wendy: It went on a long time. Almost a year of relaxation! They were trying

'Thank you, the RAH, for putting up with me for my 50th birthday celebrations. Harpists, trumpeters, tenors, sopranos, accordionists, orchestra, rock star, conductor, actor, you name it, you can be a platform for it.'

BRYN TERFEL, AFTER HIS BIRTHDAY CONCERT WITH GUESTS INCLUDING STING. DANIELLE DE NIESE AND ALISON BALSOM, OCTOBER 2015

'Visit after visit – this is the place to be! Please never turn me away!!!'

CLIFF RICHARD, 2010

'I feel like I'm on the inside of the most beautiful cake in the entire world.'

COUNTRY SINGER KACEY MUSGRAVES, 2015

'Wow! What a place! Magic in many unusual ways. The honour of this night will be with me forever.'

DEVIN TOWNSEND, AFTER PLAYING THE HALL IN APRIL 2015

'This space has been a dream for me for a long time. My mother said I would play it some day. We laughed at her. Tonight was a dream come true.'

GREGORY PORTER, AFTER HEADLINING BLUESFEST IN 2014

OPPOSITE: The Who's
Roger Daltrey and Eric
Clapton pose with their
replica paving stone stars
in front of the Royal
Albert Hall. The venue
unveiled eleven paving
stone stars dedicated to
the most famous faces
who have contributed to
the venue in the past 150
years.

OVERLEAF: Eric Clapton
performing at the Royal
Albert Hall as part of
a seven-night run of
concerts in May 2015.

*'To the Royal Albert Hall – you are my Heart! And my
Home! Your Liza.'*

LIZA MINNELLI, 2011

*'I have sometimes been asked if the location of a concert
can have an influence on a performance. For me, I can
say unequivocally that it does and it has. Over the years,
we have been blessed with performing in many beautiful,
renowned, historic and archaeologically significant
locations. These places are deeply infused with the unique
essence and energy of those who have been there before –
performers and audiences alike. This adds yet one more
dimension to our collective experience. Our evening at
the Royal Albert Hall in London was one such occasion.
I am delighted to have shared it with some extraordinary
musicians and with some of you. Thank you once again for
joining me on this part of my journey.'*

FROM LOREENA MCKENNITT'S LIVE AT THE ROYAL ALBERT HALL
ALBUM, 2019

The Stars Come Out

On 4 September 2018, the first eleven Royal Albert Hall Stars were awarded, in recognition of the people and groups who had played a key role in the venue's history. The engraved stones are topped off with a brass star, and were hand carved by Fergus Wessel. They are placed around the canopy of the building.

At their launch, Chief Executive Craig Hassall told the recipients and gathered onlookers: 'From political activists to ground-breaking artists, Churchill to charity shows, Ali to Adele, this new walk of fame recognises the unparalleled diversity of the Hall's history, and many of the unforgettable characters and events who have helped to shape this British institution.'

The inaugural Royal Albert Hall Stars are dedicated to:

Adele – Filmed record-breaking DVD *Live at the Royal Albert Hall* in 2011

Muhammad Ali – Fought in the Hall three times between 1971 and 1979

Shirley Bassey – More than forty-five appearances since 1971

BBC Proms – Resident at the Hall since 1941

Chelsea Arts Club Balls – Famous New Year's Eve extravaganzas, 1910 to 1958

Winston Churchill – Sixteen rallies between 1911 and 1959

Eric Clapton – Over 200 performances since 1964

The Who – Driving force behind Teenage Cancer Trust gigs since 2000

Albert Einstein – Campaigning for global peace, 1933

The Suffragettes – Twenty-five meetings from 1908 to 1910

Queen Victoria – Opened the Hall in memory of her husband, Prince Albert

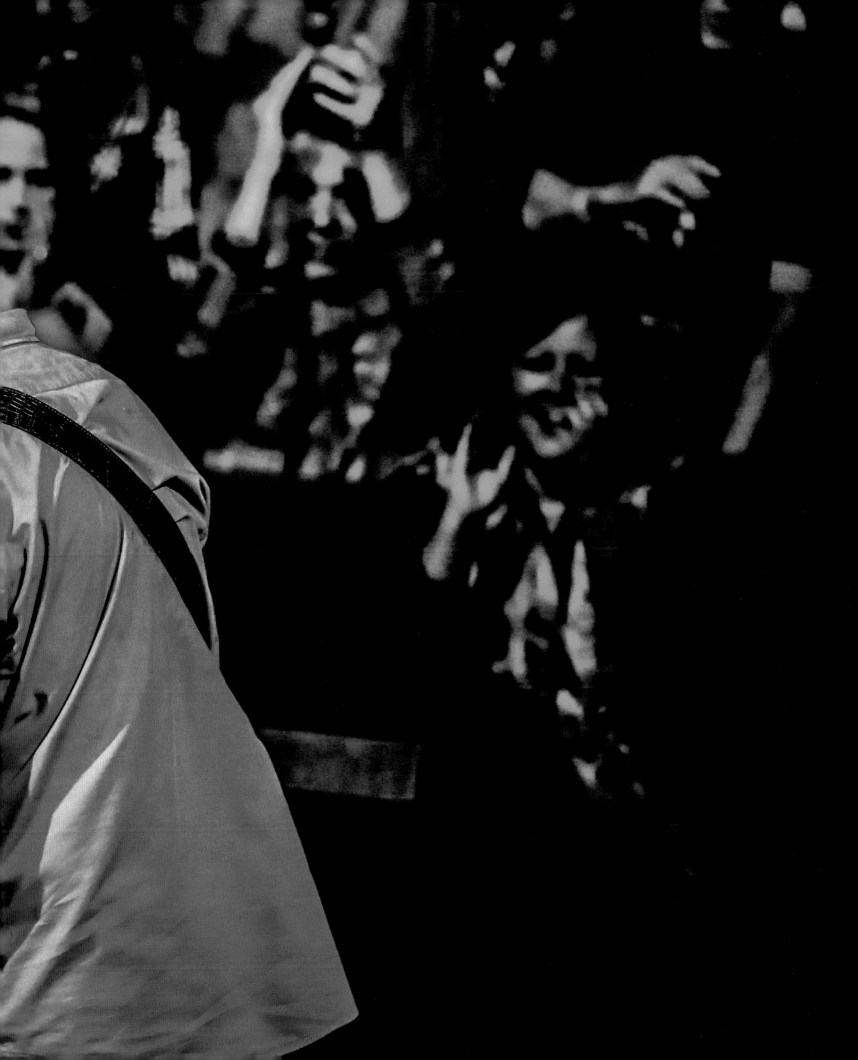

Thanks for the Memories

'Thank you for affording me the distinct honour of playing the Royal Albert Hall!!! Hope it's the first show of many.'
<small>MICHAEL BUBLÉ, 2004</small>

'To the Royal Albert Hall, a hall that made me fall in love with Great Britain. Thank you very much.'
<small>TONY BENNETT, 2012</small>

to get over to us the importance of being relaxed on stage and not being tense, as being tense can make your throat seize up, your brain seize up, you'll find yourself terrified and incapable. But if you're relaxed you can just do it. Paddy: Then we learnt to breathe. We had to swing out the ribs and be very straight. There was an invisible thread that pulled up the top of your head to the ceiling.

Paddy also remembers being taught vowel sounds using a 'bone prop', which was laid on the tongue: 'This is the phrase we would repeat: "Who would know ought of art must learn and then take his ease". The mouth started with a little "ooh", gradually getting to "aah", and then "aye".' The endless repetition of these vowel sounds made them sound 'like a lot of monkeys', she laughs.

STEAMY WINDOWS
Building services technician John McCann has worked for the Hall since the 1990s, and he has been on hand to solve many an everyday issue, from fixing toilets and mending the heating system to being called in on his day off to lower the Union Flag to half-mast on the tragic death of Princes Diana in 1997. One star's particular demand sticks in his mind: 'I remember John Denver wanted the shower extremely hot, so that he could get his voice lubricated,' he says. 'The trouble is we were turning the water up so hot that the whole flipping Hall was boiling – there was steam billowing out.'

Thanks for the Memories

OPPOSITE: Iggy Pop
crowdsurfing during his
performance for Post Pop
Depression, 13 May 2016.

'The beauty of the Hall was that one night you would have people there in dinner jackets, listening to Puccini or Verdi, and then another night you'd have the hippies, people rolling joints, and the stewards had no idea what they were in the '60s. I love the boxing at the Hall. You used to have signs all the way round the Hall in the '60s and '70s that said "No Betting Allowed", and next to the signs you'd have large men with wall-to-wall shoulders, broken noses, scared faces and camel-hair coats with huge bundles of cash peeling them off and taking bets before every fight. I saw Muhammad Ali there, I saw many of the greats: Henry Cooper, Dave Boy Green. Dave Boy Green was not one of the great rock 'n' roll boxing champions, but he had a following from the West Country and whenever he fought at the Albert Hall there would be five or six hundred men dressed as country yokels wearing smocks with straw hats, some of them carrying pitchforks. Can you imagine being allowed into the Albert Hall with a pitchfork today?'

SEATHOLDER LARRY VINER, 2017

'The most wonderful theatre altogether ... is the Royal Albert Hall – my first concert was 1968 – I am happy this evening's audience remind me of that night – thank you.'

NANA MOUSKOURI, 2014

A Brush with Greatness

Peter Reginald Pearce worked in various departments in the Hall after joining as an apprentice in the print room in 1946. One of his highlights was meeting the great activist and actor Paul Robeson:

> As I went to the different departments, I got little jobs. Paul Robeson was here to do a show and the gentleman downstairs said to me 'I've got a job for you, Pete.' Down I go with [Robeson's] letter and I knocked on the door very loud. And there was this big booming voice of Robeson, really loud and he said 'Come in,' and I walked in. He said, 'Thank you for bringing my parcel. You are a good boy,' and he gave me half a crown. I came out of there and I thought I was a millionaire!

It's a Rap

Rap star Kano first played the Hall in 2006 as a support to Jay-Z, who ended his UK tour with a special show backed by a full orchestra. Seeing how much Jay-Z loved the setting and the show, Kano had the venue at the top of his list for his Hoodies All Summer tour, and headlined in October 2019 as part of the Albert Sessions:

> The grandness of the architecture in this building and the history of the building, just walking through corridors backstage you realise the weight. Even in the [Elgar Room] the people on the wall, it's like 'wow' – such a lot of great people have played here. All of that goes into the performance. It's like you carry the weight of what's happened before onto that stage and you want to make your mark and you don't want to mess that night up. I remember [rapper] Ghetts saying to me afterwards he felt like a gladiator in there. He said it felt like the Coliseum when the crowd roars and because of the shape of the building, just how it vibrates, it's just different to anything else we've ever played before. It's 5,000 people but feels like 50,000 people. It's crazy.

Special Guest

Oscar-winning composer Michael Giacchino, who provided scores for the drama series *Lost* and for Pixar movies including *The Incredibles, Up* and *Ratatouille*, celebrated his fiftieth birthday with a gala celebration at the Hall. He was joined on the stage by directors J.J. Abrams, Pete Docter and Andrew Stanton – and one more very special guest:

'The most amazing venue in the world ... and the only place where mushrooms grow on the ceiling!'

THE BOOTLEG BEATLES, 2010

'I can't believe what just happened. #KylieChristmas at @royalalberthall was beyond amazing. A night I will never forget. THANK YOU!!!!!!'

KYLIE MINOGUE TWEETS AFTER HER SHOW IN DECEMBER 2015

'The number one dream place to play. It just doesn't get any better than here!'

RICK WAKEMAN, 2014

'To the majestic and mythical Royal Albert Hall – it was an honour to stand on your stage.'

SHERYL CROW, 2014

LEFT: Kylie Minogue
performs at A Kylie
Christmas on 9 and 10
December 2016.

'To Bertie Hall – you were marvellous, nothing can top my three nights here.'

STEPHEN FRY, 2010

'It's a beautiful place, absolutely amazing. It's overwhelming really, one of the most famous venues in the world I think and so it's a great honour to be here. When the band first formed our ambition was to play the pub down the road, I don't think we had ambitions of this grandeur. But over the last five years it's been our ambition to play here.'

MUSE SINGER MATT BELLAMY, 2013

OPPOSITE: Stephen Fry
Live, 20 September 2010.

There's no better venue than the Royal Albert Hall, it's the best in the world, and I've been so lucky to come here many times and perform. In fact, one of the greatest things I ever got to do was having my fiftieth birthday party here, when I not only got to review everything that I've written over the years but also had all my friends that worked on those films there with me. For us all to be together on the stage at my favourite hall in the world – I don't know how you ever top that. Muppet master Dave Goelz was here with Gonzo and he performed with us. I still look at that photo and can't believe that actually happened, because as a kid I loved the Muppets, they meant so much to me. Then as I grew older, I got to work with them and then became friends with many of them. To have Dave come out and perform as Gonzo here at the Hall with all of us was beyond special.

LOST IN THE SPACE

Music photographer Christie Goodwin has shot over two hundred gigs at the Royal Albert Hall:

I do remember the sensation, the emotion, because it was the first time I entered here and we were sort of let loose. I was shooting from one side and wanted to shoot from the other side and kept on running around in circles and never found the door to enter the other side that I had in my head. I remember coming home and thinking, 'I'm never doing that again!' I thought it was just impossible to work there and I needed a map to show me where to go. I am still walking around in circles but now I know every nook and cranny of the Hall.

Thanks for the Memories

Thanks for the Memories

BELOW: The exterior of
the hall lit up for the BBC
Proms, 12 July 2018.

16 HISTORY IS COMING

As the Hall reaches a remarkable milestone, staff and trustees are already looking forward to the next 150 years, with ambitious projects planned to bring the venue up to date for modern demands. These projects will enable the Hall to continue fulfilling Prince Albert's vision of a forum for shared ideas; a space to inspire artists and audiences worldwide with the magic of the iconic venue, creating life-enriching, unforgettable experiences for everyone.

150 YEARS YOUNG

An eclectic programme of entertainment, education and events has been planned to celebrate the 150th birthday of this iconic venue. The planning for the 150th birthday has been interrupted by a global pandemic that closed the doors of the Hall for the first time since WWII, leading to a degree of uncertainty about the celebrations. Planned events include a birthday parade and gala dinner; special one off concerts from past favourites to new and exciting artists a special anniversary tour; special community events which support our charitable purposes. Special concerts will celebrate the 75th birthdays of both the promoter Raymond Gubbay and the Royal Philharmonic Orchestra, and the organ's 150th birthday will be celebrated with a commission from the American composer Michael Giacchino.

In addition, a special oratorio has been commissioned from the multifaceted producer and composer Nitin Sawhney celebrating immigrants, diversity and inclusivity, and a mini-festival will accompany its debut. There will be a huge Education & Outreach project culminating in a performance on the birthday itself of a special piece composed by David Arnold, known for his work on the Bond films and the Sherlock television series. He has been working with various groups, from school children through to the elderly for this cross-generational project.

The upkeep of the Hall requires constant planning for the next stage of improvements. Between 2022 and 2026, for example, there will be an interior restoration of the entrances, stairs and corridors, and the building's floor and roof may have to be replaced.

The Great Excavation and Masterplan

The Great Exhibition of 1851 was the inspiration for Prince Albert's original concept for the Royal Albert Hall, so it is fitting that the expansion of the building has been named the Great Excavation. As well as the Great Excavation, the £35-million Masterplan, which began in 2017, involved digging down under the south-west quarter of the Hall to create a two-storey, double-height basement, providing an additional 11,200 square feet (1,040 square metres) of space. Going forward, this newly-created space will be for staff and equipment.

The south west basement will eventually have improved backstage facilities, with new dressing rooms and an artists' bar, as well as spaces for staff offices. The Hall's heating and ventilation system has also been upgraded, with the old boilers being replaced by more energy-efficient ones.

These improvements mean that the building can continue to create unforgettable experiences for artists and audiences alike. The Masterplan will run until 2031, and includes repairs to the roof, an interior restoration, a new archive and an exciting public engagement space.

'When we go back to the principals of why we exist – to promote the arts, culture and science, and also to maintain this building – we talk a lot about what "maintaining" means, and to me maintaining is not keeping the Hall as it was in 1871, it's maintaining the Hall as a contemporary, relevant performance and congregation venue,' says the Hall's CEO Craig Hassall. 'So that means the best toilets, the best seats, the best view, the best sound system, the best bars and food offers. Meeting the expectations of contemporary audiences is part of the maintenance of the Hall. I'd like to make sure that the Hall is still at the forefront of technology, in terms of entertainment venues – that it's still the place on the map, it's still the go-to for big ceremonies.'

Lost and Found

The Great Excavation threw up some fascinating historical artefacts that had been buried beneath the Hall for 150 years or more. A huge stone lion's foot – possibly from the Royal Horticultural Society's conservatory, which used to sit

BELOW: Discoveries from
The Great Excavation.

OVERLEAF: The organ in
the main auditorium of
the Royal Albert Hall, 18
November 2013.

History is Coming

The Great Excavation provides around 11,200 square feet (1,040 square metres) of additional space over two levels, with 5,600 square feet (520 square metres) of office space and 3,450 square feet (320 square metres) of storage space and a new 2,150 square foot (200 square metre) boiler house

16,236 tonnes of excavation waste, 91 per cent of which was diverted from landfill

5,480 tonnes of concrete

13.5 tonnes of plasterboard

By weight, 35 per cent of all materials were made from recycled content

Over 70 per cent of the workers on the project were from the local community (within twenty miles)

The project achieved waste neutrality, using more recycled content in the materials brought to the site than the total construction waste removed from the site

to the south of Hall – was found, along with everyday items that give a snapshot of Victorian life. As well as a clay pipe and an early Bovril jar, hundreds of oyster shells were uncovered. Although they are considered a luxury today, oysters used to be in abundant supply, with street sellers hawking them around London, and undoubtedly helping to feed the builders working on the Hall. It is estimated that Victorian-era costermongers sold around 124 million oysters a year in London, with most of them being brought up to Billingsgate Market from the Essex and Kent coasts – they were so cheap that they were given away free in pubs so that their saltiness would encourage people to buy more drink. Other items unearthed in the dig included numerous inkpots that the Museum of London has dated to between 1850 and 1860. Who knows, some may have belonged to the great architects of Albertopolis?

What would Albert do?

Going forward, the Hall's programme will continue to fulfil Prince Albert's vision of a venue for all. 'We asked ourselves what we will do beyond 2021, when the year of celebrations is over,' says Hassall, continuing:

"We started by going right back to Albert's founding principles, asking, 'What did Albert want from this building?' He had a vision for Albertopolis, and the Royal Albert Hall is the jewel in the crown at the top of the estate. It most properly represents what Albert wanted in terms of a legacy for the Great Exhibition, which was a forum for the sharing and dissemination of arts and science. He didn't want a theme park, he wanted something that perpetuates that sharing of both ideas and information. In terms of programming beyond 2021, there is potential for a slight shift towards more spoken-word events, more debates, more lectures and more presentations, which are a few ideas being kicked around. But never fear, there will still be lots of rock and pop shows, classical concerts, wrestling and tennis and all the things that make up the eclectic nature of the Royal Albert Hall."

For Louise Halliday, director of external affairs, the future will reflect Prince Albert's love of innovation: 'The Great Exhibition was all about showing the most up-to-date things in industry, science, the arts and the creative world generally, so we never want to become ossified or end up as a museum. We want that spirit of innovation, creativity, drive and democracy to take us into the next 150 years.'

The People's Palace

'The Royal Albert Hall to me represents one of the best examples of British culture, in that it's grand and diverse, but it's also accessible,' says Hassall. 'It's a bonkers place. It's always been this incredible melting pot of different kinds of entertainment – of debates, lectures, information sharing, celebrations and ceremonies – and it still is today. I've worked in opera, theatre, ballet and the Olympics, and there's been a bit of a common thread through those roles, which is about demystifying the performing arts, taking them off the pedestal that they are perceived to be on, making them as accessible and wide-reaching as possible. The Royal Albert Hall does that tenfold. It's such a beloved British institution, and it's really special for all the artists and performers, including children, and for the audience members who come here, and yet it's for everyone. So it has a real duality of access and specialness. It really is the people's palace.'

BELOW: Audience in the main auditorium of the Royal Albert Hall, 8 October 2014.

OVERLEAF: Coldplay performing live on the first of two nights at the Royal Albert Hall.

Index

Page references in *italics* indicate images.

Photography credits:

PRELIMS:
David Iliff: 1
Andy Paradise: 3

CHAPTER 2:
Andy Paradise: 34
Chris Christodoulou: 35
Christie Goodwin: 28,29

CHAPTER 3:
Christie Goodwin: 42
Andy Paradise: 38, 40, 41, 44

CHAPTER 4:
Christie Goodwin: 62
Paul Sanders: 50
Chris Christodoulou: 52, 53
Annabel Moeller: 64, 65, 68
Andy Paradise: 54, 55, 58, 67, 69, 70

CHAPTER 5:
Christie Goodwin: 100
Peter Blake: 82, 83
Andy Paradise: 94, 98, 99, 107

CHAPTER 6:
Paul Sanders: 134, 135
Andy Paradise: 112, 122, 126, 129
Chris Christodoulou: 118, 123, 130

CHAPTER 7:
Andy Paradise: 161
Chris Christodoulou: 148, 153, 158

CHAPTER 10:
Annabel Moeller: 192
Christie Goodwin: 206
Chris Christodoulou: 199, 200
Paul Sanders: 194, 196, 203, 205

CHAPTER 12:
Chris Christoloudou: 232
Christie Goodwin: 230, 233, 239
Andy Paradise: 226, 235, 236, 237

CHAPTER 13:
Andy Paradise: 260
Christie Goodwin: 254
Chris Christoloudou: 264, 266

CHAPTER 14:
Christie Goodwin: 276
Paul Sanders: 272, 273
Andy Paradise: 266, 269, 274, 278

CHAPTER 15:
Chris Christoloudou: 290
Justin Ng: 287
Andy Paradise: 280, 283, 299
Christie Goodwin: 282, 288, 289,
292, 296

CHAPTER 16:
J Collingridge: 306, 307
Christie Goodwin: 309
Andy Paradise: 300,303, 304

All other images © the Royal Albert
Hall from their archive

Ebury and the Royal Albert Hall
have made every attempt to trace the
creators of the assets in this book.
If you have a legitimate claim to
copyright of any images in the book,
or have any copyright information
that will be useful to us, please
contact the marketing department at
the Royal Albert Hall.

Acknowledgements:

CRAIG HASSALL
ANTHONY WINTER-BROWN
LOUISE HALLIDAY
ANTHONY LYNCH
ELIZABETH HARPER
MATT GRIFFIN

NATHAN LAMB
SUZANNE KEYTE
ALICIA KIRKBRIDE
FLO SCHROEDER
OLLIE JEFFREY
STEPHANIE BALDWIN

ED COBBOLD
LIZ HARPER
MATTHEW MANN
RUTH SANDERS

1 2 3 4 5 6 7 8 9 10

Published in 2020 by Ebury Press an imprint of Ebury Publishing,
20 Vauxhall Bridge Road,
London SW1V 2SA

Ebury Press is part of the Penguin Random House group of companies
whose addresses can be found at global.penguinrandomhouse.com

Text © The Royal Albert Hall 2020
Design © Ebury Press 2020

The Royal Albert Hall have asserted their right to be identified as the author of this
Work in accordance with the Copyright, Designs and Patents Act 1988

This edition published by Ebury Press in 2020

www.penguin.co.uk

A CIP catalogue record for this book is available from the British Library

Designed by David Rowley
Text by Alison Maloney
Publishing Director: Carey Smith
Editor: Camilla Ackley

ISBN 9781529103748

Printed and bound in Italy

MIX
Paper from
responsible sources
FSC® C018179
www.fsc.org